Sew Today's Fashions

for 18-inch dolls

Götz and American Girl dolls

Joan Hinds

Published by

An imprint of F+W Publications, Inc.

700 East State Street • Iola, WI 54990-0001
715-445-2214 • 888-457-2873
www.krause.com

Our toll-free number to place an order or obtain a free catalog is 800-258-0929.

Dolls pictured on the cover (from left to right):
Laura Ashley®, Springfield Collection®, and American Girl®.

The following registered trademark terms and companies appear in this publication:
Aleene's® Clear Gel Tacky Glue®, American Girl® by Pleasant Company, Collector's Lane®, Crafter's Pick: The Ultimate®, Creative Doll Company®, Creative Versa-tool®, Dritz for Dolls®, Easy Bleach® by Prym-Dritz, Exact-o®, Fabri-tac®, Götz™, Lycra®, Our Generation™, Springfield Collection®, Tolly Girl®, Ultrasuede®, and Velcro®.

Library of Congress Catalog Number: 2004093869

ISBN: 0-87349-772-4

Edited by Sarah Herman
Designed by Donna Mummery

Printed in the United States of America

13 12 11 10   7 6 5 4

Dedication

To good friends.

Acknowledgments

I wish to express a huge thank you to the many talented people who helped me with the design concepts and project completion in this book! I couldn't have done it alone!

Many thanks go to:

My good friends Marilee Sagat, her daughter Stivi Sagat, Lauri Cushing, and Ceci Riehl, who offered invaluable design assistance and helped with many projects, especially the knitted and embroidered clothing.

My skilled photographer, Tigg, who has extraordinary patience and vision with 18-inch dolls.

My fabulous illustrator, Kathy Marsaa, who always explains my creations with exceptional visual clarity.

The enthusiastic staff at Krause Publications, including Julie, Niki, and Sarah, who helped me make my wardrobe ideas for today's dolls a reality.

Lastly, my husband Fletcher, who patiently helps with crucial design questions and proofreads whenever I need his help.

Creative Doll Company, Götz, and Laura Ashley dolls

Göiz doll

Table of Contents

Introduction

Children have enjoyed dressing their dolls since the beginning of time. They especially love to dress them in clothing that mimics their own styles. Today, those styles are the clothing that preteens wear. This ranges from jeans of all types to t-shirts, sports clothing, and dresses.

I have designed this book to include patterns for all types of clothing for 18-inch dolls. 30 outfits have been designed with the preteen girl in mind. These outfits span the activities that preteen girls participate in, such as school, sports, outdoor activities, shopping, and dress-up special occasions.

Clothing for girls today is smooth and sleek, but often has a soft feminine side with ruffles and sheer overskirts. Influence from the 60s and 70s is evident with flared pant legs, wide belts, neck ruffles, and thick platform shoes. Even polyester double-knit is making a big comeback for pants and skirts! Sleeves are fitted over the upper arm and almost never have any gathers in the sleeve caps. They can, however, flare out after the elbow. Fitted shirts usually come only to the waist and are often worn with low-waisted jeans and pants, known as "hip huggers" in my generation. Please note, however, that no belly buttons are shown in this book! Dresses are still worn, usually for special occasions. Soft full skirts are combined with fitted bodices in today's wardrobe.

Jeans and t-shirts are the hottest type of clothing for girls. The jeans, made from all kinds of denim or twill, are decorated and accented in many different ways. Belts are a fashion must nowadays. They are usually wide with fringe, eyelets, or linked leather shapes. The pant legs have much decoration with embroidery, bleaching techniques, or jeweled appliqués. The t-shirts are also highly decorated with embroidery and jewels. I designed similar trendy casual wear for dolls. They are shown with several types of jeans, shorts, and capri pants. Most of them have a flared bottom with embroidery, insets, and jewels. The tops have the same types of embellishments. You can make each outfit

your own by trimming clothing items with custom embellishments. Jewels can be used to accent embroidery and belts are interchangeable.

School clothing today can be classic, such as pleated skirts and button down collar shirts, or casual pants and tops. Knitted sweaters and vests for dolls combine easily with the skirts and pants. The ever-popular varsity jacket, often seen on today's campuses, looks great in any color combination.

Children participate in many sports activities that have uniforms or special clothing requirements. Warm-up suits of all kinds are worn off the field and as casual clothing. Dolls can have uniforms for soccer and basketball sewn in their team colors. Competition costumes for skating activities can be customized to match their human counterparts.

Cute casual dresses for girls can be scaled down for dolls. Denim and twill fabrics are popular choices for these dresses. Ruffles and appliqués are popular motifs on prints and solid color fabrics. More formal attire is reserved for special occasions such as First Communion, holiday parties, or weddings. You can make similar costumes for your dolls to commemorate these events in girls' lives.

Outerwear is often made of fleece, one of today's most popular fabrics. Dolls need a jacket and a vest made from fleece, along with a hat and scarf. It is easy to sew and can be decorated simply with an outline stitch or embroidery. Fleece-backed outerwear fabric is making a comeback today. Jackets can be made quickly using this fabric. Don't forget knitted scarves, mittens, and caps. The cap, called a beanie in today's wardrobe, fits quite tightly and is pulled down on the forehead.

Lastly, sleepwear takes the usual form in pajamas and nightgowns. The difference today is the fabrics. Flannel-backed satin is very popular for all types of nightwear. Traditional flannel is still seen in funky new prints.

Accessories have been said to "make the outfit." Adding belts, shoulder bags, jewelry, and caps will give your fashions the fun, trendy look of today.

Which Dolls Will These Patterns Fit?

The American Girl doll by Pleasant Company took the doll market by storm in the 1980s. With this rebirth of child-like play dolls, other manufacturers created their own brands of 18-inch vinyl dolls. The faces are all unique, but the cloth bodies are sufficiently similar to exchange clothing, particularly dresses. Arms and legs sometimes vary enough to require different sleeve and pant lengths, but most of them can wear the clothing in this book.

Even within a single brand, stuffed cloth bodies may vary from doll to doll. The bodies don't come from a mold and there is a human element involved in their fullness. Also, dolls that remain in stands or are actively played with may become slimmer over time. In most cases, the most critical measurement is the waist. The patterns in this book presume an 11½" waist. This measurement is most important when making garments with a waistband.

The dolls pictured in this book are from a variety of manufacturers. In the case of Collector's Lane, Tolly Girl Doll Company, and the Springfield Collection dolls, be sure to make note that the arms and legs are slightly narrower and the waist measurements are usually smaller than the American Girl doll. The Creative Doll Company doll has slightly wider hips and needs more depth in the crotch area.

As long as this type of doll remains popular, more brands will appear each year. Be aware that they may need slight adjustments in waistbands, hem, sleeve lengths, etc.

How Do I Make These Fitting Adjustments?

The best way to insure a perfect fit for your particular doll is to make a trial muslin for at least the bodice or shirt. This way you can accurately see how well the garment will fit. It is helpful if you have the doll you are sewing for in your possession while you make her clothing. Try on each garment as you are sewing to make sure that you have the proper fit.

If your doll is slimmer than the American Girl doll, you will probably need to adjust the waist. If the garment has elastic in the waistband, you can shorten the elastic length to make it fit. If you are making the Low-Rise Jeans from this book, the pants have no waistband. The pants are open at the back and just meet at center back with Velcro. For a slimmer doll, you can overlap the center back edges before you sew the Velcro in place. If the bodice or shirt is too full, take a small amount off the side seams or the center back seam before finishing the garment.

If your doll has wider hips or a deeper crotch, such as the Creative Doll Company doll, making a trial muslin for the pants will be helpful. The curve in the crotch area may need to be lengthened.

Most dolls will not be thicker in the waist than the 11½" measurement. If you need to add width to the clothing, adding a small amount to the side seams under the armholes will usually suffice. To widen pants at the waist, add a small amount to the top of the pants pattern pieces, and be sure to lengthen the waistband.

Taking a little extra time while you are sewing your doll's wardrobe is always a good idea. This will ensure you are satisfied with the results.

Before You Begin

Now that you have decided to sew a wonderful new wardrobe for your doll, you will be anxious to get started. But first I must say a few words about general sewing instructions. Please read this section carefully before you begin.

Measurements of your doll are an absolute must. Start a chart of all the pertinent measurements you might need. These are: waist, upper arm, wrist, neck and ankle circumference, back shoulder width, and back neck-to-crotch length. A new narrow tape measure is available to help you with this task. It is narrow enough to wrap around the smallest of doll parts.

Top row: Tally Girl and Götz dolls
Bottom row: American Girl dolls

Five dolls wearing various tops and bottoms.

The same five dolls with the same separates that have been mixed and matched to create five completely different outfits.

Top row: American Girl and Tolly Girl dolls
Bottom row: American Girl, American Girl, and Götz dolls

Gather all your equipment. Begin with a sewing machine, sewing shears, pins, seam gauge, and washout marker. A serger is not necessary, even for the knit garments, but it helps with construction and gives seam allowances a clean finish. A steam iron is a must. There is a "mini-iron" designed for the quilting industry that is also perfect for the small areas in doll clothing construction. Small ironing boards are essential for pressing small sleeves, collars, pant legs, etc.

The next step is to decide which garment or separates you will want to make. I have categorized the outfits by the activities in a young girl's life. Casual wear was put in the shopping, picnic, and playground categories, but the outfits can be worn for any purpose you like. I also needed to put the separates together to make a complete outfit for each doll. You, however, can put them together in countless ways to make many more outfits. A sweater can look nice with capri pants or with a skirt. Jeans can be worn with any type of t-shirt, jacket, shirt, or sweater.

Don't hesitate to try your own mixing and matching! You can see that many different combinations are possible with the patterns in the book.

Choosing fabrics has always been one of my favorite parts of sewing for dolls. Denim is still as hot as ever, and comes in many shades and even a few patterns. Be sure to get the lightest weight you can find for doll garments. If the denim is too heavy, your garments will be stiff and may look bulky. Knit fabrics are perfect for t-shirts, swimwear, and athletic costumes. Fleece remains a popular fabric for jackets, caps, scarves, and sportswear. You can't ask much more from this fabric, since it is easy to sew, doesn't ravel, and doesn't wrinkle.

For dressy clothes, satin and sheer organza are always a good choice. Stretch velvet is wonderful for the holidays when it is paired with full, gathered skirts. School clothes look great when made from wool or a cotton flannel look-a-like.

Try one of the new fabrics available, such as fleece-backed suede for outerwear.

Embellishment techniques can be the icing on the cake. They can make common garments such as jeans or shirts into your own unique fashion statement. The techniques given for one particular outfit can be used on any of the others. The jeans can be the most fun to decorate, since anything goes these days. I have included embroidery, jewels, eyelets, fabric insets, and a bleaching technique with stencils. You can also try appliqué, painting, hand embroidery, lace or iron-on appliqués, and so much more. Don't be afraid of a new idea or technique. The sky's the limit!

Please note that all seam allowances are ¼" unless specified otherwise. We have become accustomed to using a ⅝" seam allowance for garment sewing, so the transition to narrower seams may take a little effort. Some of us tend to make the seams slightly wider than ¼". This may affect the fit. An easy way to be sure you have accurate seam allowances is to use a quilting presser foot that has a width of ¼" built in. Be aware that the foot has a small hole, so you cannot zigzag stitch without switching presser feet. Another option is to use an edge stitching foot. If your sewing machine can adjust the needle position from side-to-side, you can move the needle so that the stitching will be exactly ¼" from the fabric edge.

Most of the garments that close in the back have an overlap of approximately ½". While it is always safer to have the particular doll you are sewing for in front of you, if you are sewing for a doll not in your possession, this is a measurement to note.

T-shirts are made from knit fabrics with a horizontal stretch. Some sewers have had trouble fitting the shirts over the doll's head if the fabric or ribbing does not adequately stretch. The t-shirts in this book are designed to have a center back seam that opens part or all the way down the back. (One exception is the short-sleeved t-shirt that opens at the shoulder seam.) Therefore, the shirts will fit over the doll's head, no matter how much stretch the knit has.

Seam finishes are only mentioned when absolutely necessary. Feel free to finish the seam allowances as you prefer,

either with a serger or zigzag stitching. Some machines have a three-step zigzag, which allows the fabric to be stitched without rolling or bunching. I have finished the garments in this book with Velcro strips, but you can substitute snaps if you prefer.

Lastly, accessories help pull the outfit together. I have instructions for several, including sandals. Sandals are quite easy to make with soles made from craft foam. The thinner material is cut with a scissors, but the thicker foam needs to be cut with a craft or hot knife. The thicker sole may be a little rougher on the edges than if it was die-cut, but still works well. You can use any materials for the straps across the top. Even a length of grosgrain ribbon will look great. Straps can be accented on the top with beads, ribbon, flowers, or craft foam shapes.

Necklaces are a fabulous way to personalize your doll's wardrobe. Instructions are included for a 70s-style hemp macramé necklace and a simple ribbon choker. You can make the other chain necklaces shown in the photos as well. Initials are a hot fashion theme today. You can find tiny inexpensive initials in jewelry stores to hang on a chain. Tiny jeweled shapes such as hearts or stars are also popular. If you don't have a metal chain, they can be purchased in craft stores and shortened for your doll's neck.

Hand or shoulder bags are a big fashion statement. The bags in the book are shoulder bags, but the straps can be shortened to make them handbags. Any material can be used to decorate them just like the jeans.

Making Sweaters and Other Hand Knits for Dolls

Knitting has become increasingly popular in the last decade, and your dolls hope you get in the act, too. I have included instructions for sweaters, mittens, hats, and a scarf for you to try. One of the hats is felted, which means it is knit in a larger size, washed in hot water, and shaped to fit the doll's head.

The sweaters are styles seen in ready-to-wear for girls today. The stylish zipper-front cardigans seem to be worn everywhere, and cable knits are also very

popular. Usually these garments will fit all the 18-inch dolls without much alteration. If you use a different type of yarn than the type given in the supply list, work up a small sample to be sure that the gauge remains the same.

The knitted cap shown in this book is a close fitting cap called a "beanie" by girls today. It is the perfect solution for a bad hair day. It is paired with a long striped scarf and garter stitch mittens. Girls wear the cap or scarf with any indoor outfit, and your doll can, too.

Before you begin knitting, I have included a few general terms and guidelines for knitting the patterns in this book. They are as follows:

St(s): Stitch(es).

Psso: Pass slipped stitch over the stitch immediately left of it on the right hand needle and drop it (a decrease slanting left).

K2 tog: Knit two stitches together as one (a decrease slanting right).

Ssk : (Slip, slip, knit) Slip two stitches, one at a time as if to knit; slide left needle through the front loops of these slipped stitches, from left to right, and knit them together from this position (a decrease slanting left).

Sk2po: Slip one stitch, knit 2, pass slipped stitch over last one on needle (3 stitches decreased to 1).

M1: (Make one) Insert left needle, from front to back, under the horizontal strand between last stitch worked and next stitch on left needle, forming a loop on needle. Knit through the back of this loop.

Yo: (Yarn over) Pass yarn over needle as if to knit (1 stitch added which will create a hole).

Pm: Place marker.

Stockinette stitch: Knit all stitches on the outside. Purl all stitches on the inside.

Knit the knits and purl the purls: On the inside of the work, a stitch that was knitted on the outside looks like a purl. If you purl this stitch on the inside, it will look like a knit stitch on the outside. This term means work the opposite stitch on the inside so that from the outside it looks the same as the stitch below it. It is just a confusing way of stating something very simple.

K1, p1 rib: On the outside, repeat (k1, p1) across. On the inside, knit the knits and purl the purls.

K2, p2 rib: On the outside, repeat (k2, p2) across. On the inside, knit the knits and purl the purls.

W&T: Wrap and turn. Bring yarn to the front of the work. Slip one stitch. Bring yarn to the back of the work. Slip the stitch back to the left needle. Turn. This eliminates a hole at the turning point.

Pick up and knit: Insert the right needle into the edge of the work under one or two firm strands; wrap yarn around the needle as if to knit and pull the loop through, creating a new loop on the left needle.

Bind off and join: This is an easy and neat way to finish the shoulder seam. Line up both points of the needle with the stitches to be bound off, so that the front and back of the sweater are on top of each other, outsides together. Using a second needle or a crochet hook and the working yarn, or the 24" tail that is hanging there, bring a loop through the last loop on both needles. That is, insert the hook or needle as if to knit into the last loop on the front needle and then the last loop on the back needle and pull the loop through both. Pull one stitch off each needle. Repeat this step with the next two stitches. Now pull the first stitch on the right hand needle over the second, or if using a crochet hook, pull the second stitch through the first. Give this stitch an extra tug to be sure it doesn't get too tight. Continue in this manner until all stitches from the sweater front have been used up.

Shop 'Til You Drop, Part I

Girls love to hang out at the mall, and so do their dolls. The dolls shown here wear some of the latest fashions while they shop. One outfit is a t-shirt with cuffs, a fleece vest, and jeans with a bleached-out star motif on the pant legs. The long-sleeved t-shirt has circular cuffs with a "lettuce" edge, a popular decorative technique for today's knits. Pulling the fabric slightly as you stitch with a wide zigzag stitch makes the knit edges ripple. Her vest is made from fleece, another fashion staple. The zipper only opens to the yoke in front and the edges are bound by packaged fleece binding. You could also use Lycra binding. The design motif in the fleece is stars, which is echoed on the jeans. Before the jeans are constructed, a bleaching process is applied to the fabric using a stencil. You can find many stencil designs to use, such as hearts, bugs, flowers, etc. Be sure to follow the manufacturer's instructions when using chemicals on fabric. Make her necklace using an initial found in the girls' jewelry section of stores. It is placed on a silver chain from craft stores, shortened to an 8" length with clasps applied to both ends.

The second outfit is a fun look with a striped t-shirt and jeans with an inset at the side seams. The outfit includes a fringed belt, newsboy cap, and shoulder bag. The t-shirt has a front opening with snaps, but the t-shirt also opens in the back so children can easily put it on the doll. Her jeans are cut so they fit slightly below the waist. They have no waistband, with Velcro at the back opening. The belt, cap, and shoulder bag are hot fashion accessories. The suede belt is fringed at one end and is sewn over a metal ring on the other. The suede is sold as a pre-cut ½" strip. The cap is easier than it looks. The eight sections are stitched together and sewn to the brim in the front and band in the back. The bag can be embroidered with your own sewing machine or decorated with a purchased embroidered initial.

The last doll wears a zippered-front cable knit sweater with black double-knit pants. Black double-knit seems to be everywhere in girls' fashions today. The pants, which can also be made of woven fabric, pair perfectly with the bright lavender sweater. The sweater is hand knit on a circular needle with a separating zipper applied by hand after the knitting is completed.

T-Shirt with Cuffs, Fleece Vest and Flared Star Jeans with Yoke

Tolly Girl doll

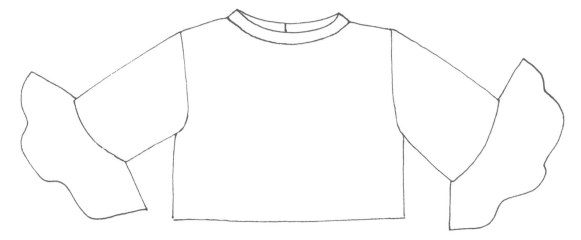

Supplies:
¼ yd. knit fabric
1½" x 8½" piece of knit ribbing
3" Velcro strip

1 Cut one front, two backs, two sleeves, and two cuffs from the knit fabric.

2 With right sides together, sew the backs to the front at the shoulder seams.

3 Fold the center back edges ¼" to the wrong side and stitch.

T-Shirt with Cuffs

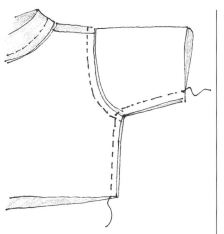

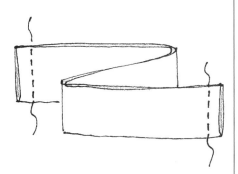

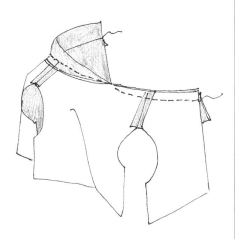

4 Fold the ribbing in half lengthwise with right sides together. Stitch the short ends and turn to the right side.

Stretching the ribbing to fit the neckline, stitch the ribbing to the neckline.

5 With right sides together, sew the sleeve caps to the armholes, easing as necessary. Stitch the underarm seam from the sleeve edges to the bottom of the shirt.

6 Set your sewing machine for a wide zigzag stitch (4.0). Stitch around the outside of the cuffs, pulling the fabric slightly and making sure the needle goes off the fabric on the right hand side.

Sew the cuffs to the sleeve edges with right sides together. Press the seam allowances toward the sleeves.

7 Press the lower edge of the shirt ½" to the wrong side and stitch.

8 Lapping right over left, sew the Velcro to the back opening.

Götz doll

Fleece Vest

Supplies:

¼ yd. fleece print fabric

1 yd. fleece or Lycra binding (1½" wide)

4" zipper (use a 7" skirt zipper and cut off the excess)

1 Cut one lower front, two upper fronts, one back, and one collar from the fabric.

2 With right sides together, sew the back to the upper fronts at the shoulders.

3 Sew one long edge of the collar to the neck edge of the jacket with right sides together. Serge or zigzag stitch the other long edge of the collar.

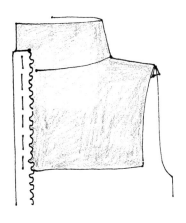

4 Measure 4" from the top of the zipper. Place the wrong side of the zipper along the left side of the front opening with the 4" mark flush with the bottom edge of the upper front. (The zipper will only extend up approximately one half of the collar width.) Baste the zipper ¼" from the front edge. Open out the zipper to the right side and pin ¼" from the stitched seam, folding the collar to the inside over the zipper and covering the jacket/collar seam. Stitch, using an edge-stitching presser foot or zipper foot.

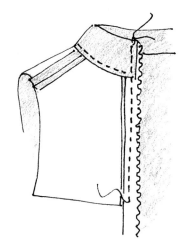

Repeat with the other side of the jacket and zipper.

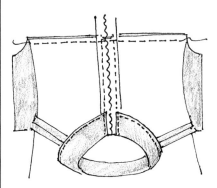

5 Sew the lower front to the upper fronts. Cut off the excess zipper. Reinforce the zipper part of the seam.

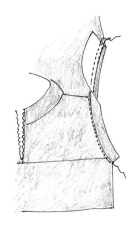

6 With right sides together, pin one edge of the fleece or Lycra strip on the seam line of an armhole. Stitch along the seam line and cut off the extra. Fold the strip to the wrong side

of the armhole and pin. Stitch over the previous seam on the right side, making sure to catch the strip underneath. Trim the strip close to the stitching on the wrong side. Repeat with the other armhole.

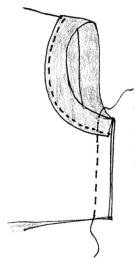

7 With right sides together, sew the side seams.

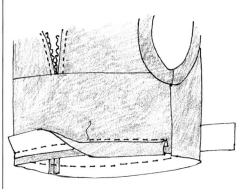

8 Pin the remaining strip of fleece or Lycra to the right side of the vest ¼" above the lower edge. Overlap the strips slightly where the strips meet and stitch just to ¼" from the end of the overlapped strip. Fold the strip to the wrong side and pin, tucking in the raw end. Stitch over the previous seam on the right side, making sure to catch the strip underneath.

TIP

The fleece vest has a zipper that only opens part of the way down on the front. The vest may be tight when children try to put it on. The best way to put the vest on the doll is to put her arms straight up in the air while putting it over the head. The arms can slip in the armholes while they pull it down.

Flared Star Jeans with Yoke

Supplies:
⅓ yd. denim fabric
11" elastic (¼" wide)
Contrasting thread for topstitching, if desired
Easy Bleach by Prym-Dritz
Star stencils in 3 sizes (1", 1¼", and 1½")
Foam stencil applicator

1 Cut two front yokes, two lower fronts, two backs, and one waistband from the fabric.

2 Following the manufacturer's instructions, use the Easy Bleach to stencil the stars on the front pant legs of the jeans. Refer to the photograph for placement. Let dry before proceeding.

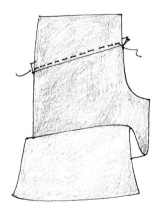

3 With right sides together, stitch the front yokes to the lower fronts. Press seam allowances to the top. With contrasting thread, topstitch a scant ⅛" above the seam.

4 Sew the center front and back seams and the side seams with right sides together.

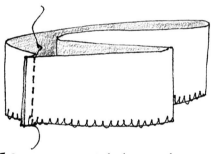

5 Serge or zigzag stitch along one long edge of the waistband. Stitch the short ends with right sides together. Press the seam allowances open.

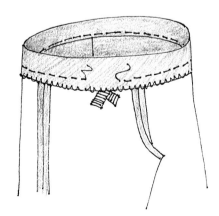

6 With right sides together, place the waistband on the jeans so that the seam of the waistband aligns with the center back seam of the jeans. Stitch. Fold the waistband over to the inside of the jeans so the waistband is ½" wide. Topstitch in place, leaving a 1" opening at the back. Thread the elastic through the casing and secure the ends. Topstitch the opening closed.

7 Serge or zigzag stitch along the lower edges of the jeans. Press the edges ½" to the wrong side. Stitch ⅜" from the pressed edge.

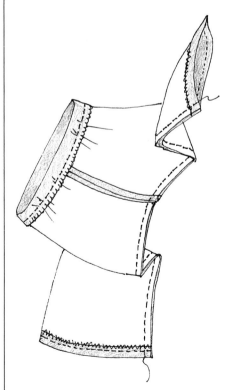

8 With right sides together, sew the inner leg seam.

Striped T-Shirt, Low-Rise Flared Jeans with Insets and Fringed Belt

Springfield Collection doll

Striped T-Shirt

Supplies:
¼ yd. striped t-shirt knit fabric

15" single-fold bias tape

1 package snaps, any color*

Snap setter tool

2½" Velcro strip

*Used in this project: Dritz for Dolls

1 Cut one front, two backs, and two sleeves from the fabric.

2 Press the center back edges ¼" to the wrong side and stitch.

3 With right sides together, sew the backs to the front at the shoulder seams.

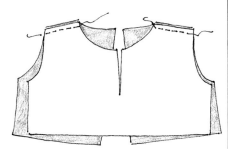

4 Slash 2½" down the center front of the shirt with a scissors. Cut two pieces of bias tape 3" long. Unfold and pin the right side of one edge of the bias tape to the wrong side of the left front slashed edge. The end of the tape should be flush with the bottom of the slash. Stitch with a ⅛" seam allowance. Fold the tape over to the right side and stitch close to the folded edge. Make sure that the width of the tape measures ⅜". Trim off any excess tape at the top of the placket, if necessary.

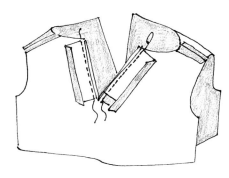

For the right front slashed edge, press one end the other piece of bias tape ¼" to the wrong side. With the pressed end

at the bottom of the placket, unfold and pin the right side of the tape to the wrong side of the slashed edge.

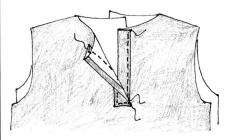

Fold the tape over to the right side and stitch along the sides and bottom end of the tape, catching the left placket underneath the stitching along the bottom only.

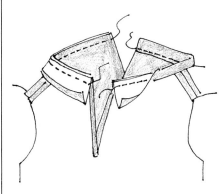

5 Unfold and pin the right side of one edge of the bias tape to the wrong side of the shirt neckline. The tape should extend ¼" beyond the center front and back edges. Stitch. Fold the tape over to the right side, tucking in the short ends. Stitch.

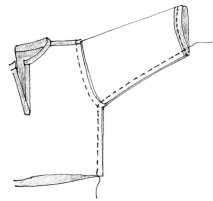

6 Press the lower edges of the sleeves ¼" to the wrong side and stitch. With right sides together, sew the sleeve caps to the armholes, easing as necessary. Sew the underarm seam from the wrist edge to the bottom of the shirt.

7 Press the hem edge ¼" to the wrong side and stitch.

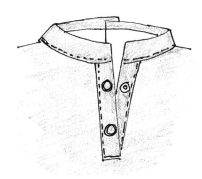

8 Using the snap setter tool, apply two snaps to the front opening of the shirt. Instead of using the flat colored snap tops, use two extra rings for the top of the snaps on the right side. The first snap should be placed ¾" from the neckline edge, and the second should be placed 1" below the first.

9 Lapping right over left, sew the Velcro to the back opening.

TIP

The snaps on the striped t-shirt are sold in packages with a solid color front. I chose to use the snap ring that is placed on the underside of a snap half also on the front. This type of snap is popular with girls' shirts today. If you choose to do this, you will have to discard the top and use a second ring from the package. You won't have as many pairs of snaps this way, so be sure to purchase enough.

Low-Rise Flared Jeans with Insets

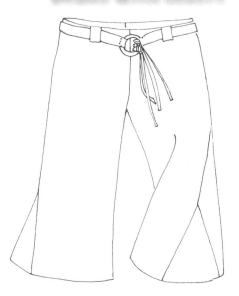

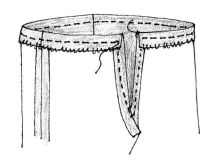

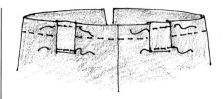

Supplies:
⅓ yd. lightweight denim fabric
Scrap of contrasting fabric for insets
1¾" Velcro strip

1 Cut two fronts, two backs, and one belt loop from the denim fabric. Cut two insets from the contrasting fabric.

2 Sew the side seams with right sides together.

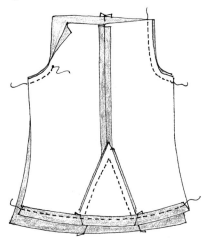

3 With right sides together, sew the insets to the lower pant legs. Serge or zigzag stitch the lower edges of the pants and press ½" to the wrong side. Stitch ⅜" from the fold.

4 With right sides together, sew the center front seam. Sew the center back seam to the dot marked on the pattern piece. Press the seam allowances open and topstitch around the open area of the seam.

5 Serge or zigzag stitch the top edge of the pants and press ½" to the wrong side. Stitch ⅜" from the fold.

 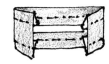

6 Press the long edges of the belt loop ¼" to the wrong side and stitch close to each folded edge. Cut in half widthwise. Press each raw end ¼" to the wrong side.

Pin one belt loop to the top of the pants as marked on the pattern piece. The folded edge of the belt loop should be flush with the top edge of the pants. Stitch close to the folded edge on each end of the loop. Repeat with the remaining belt loop on the other side.

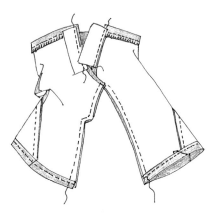

7 Sew the loop side of the Velcro to the left center back opening. One long side should be placed a scant ⅛" under the edge of the opening. Sew the hook side of the Velcro to the other back opening. The entire piece of Velcro is stitched on the wrong side of the back opening. When the pants are closed, the back opening edges will meet, but not overlap.

8 With right sides together, sew the inner leg seam.

Fringed Belt

Supplies:
½ yd. piece of suede trim (½" wide)
1 brass ring (1" diameter)

1 Fold one end of the suede ½" over the ring and stitch.

2 Make fringe at the other end of the suede by cutting close to one side for 6". Make three more cuts so the belt will have five fringed pieces.

3 Put the belt in the belt loops and tie it around the ring at the front.

Newsboy Cap and Shoulder Bag with Initial

Springfield Collection doll

Newsboy Cap

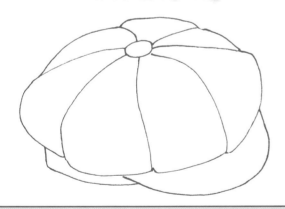

Supplies:

¼ yd. light- to medium-weight fabric

Scrap of medium-weight interfacing for cap brim

2" elastic (¼" wide)

1 button to cover (½" or ⁷⁄₁₆"), optional

40 wt. machine embroidery thread and stabilizer or
an iron-on embroidered initial (¾" wide)

1 Cut eight cap crowns, two brims, and one riser from the fabric. Cut one brim from the interfacing.

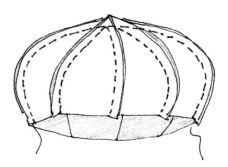

2 With right sides together, sew the eight crown sections together along the sides. They will all meet at a point at the top.

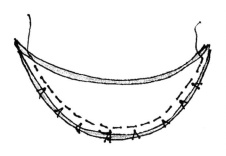

3 Baste the brim interfacing to the wrong side of one of the brims. Trim the interfacing close to the stitching. With right sides together, sew the brims together along the outside curved edge. Clip the curves, turn to the right side, and press. Topstitch around the outside stitched edge.

4 Center the brim on one of the crown sections with right sides together. Stitch.

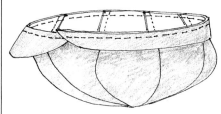

5 Press the riser in half lengthwise with wrong sides together. Place the riser on the edge of the cap with right sides together. The ends of the riser will overlap onto the brim. Bring the ends up to the seam line so that the raw ends will be included in the seam. Stitch.

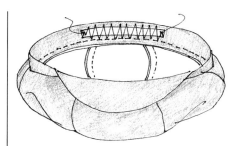

6 Find the crown section directly opposite of the brim. Stretch the elastic as much as you can and stitch it with a wide zigzag stitch to that portion of the riser.

7 If desired, cover the button with leftover fabric, following the manufacturer's instructions. Sew it to the top of the cap.

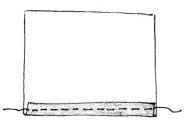

Shoulder Bag

1 If you will be embroidering an initial on the flap of your bag, stitch it with the 40 wt. thread and stabilizer before cutting out the shoulder bag. The initial shown here is ¾" high and is placed in the right corner of the flap. Otherwise, cut one back with flap, one flap lining, one front, and one strap from the fabric.

2 Press the straight edges of the flap lining and the front ¼" to the wrong side and stitch.

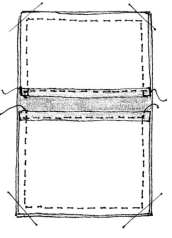

3 With right sides together, sew the flap lining to the top of the back with flap on the unstitched sides and top edges. Sew the front to the bottom of the back with flap in the same manner. Clip the curves; turn to the right side and press.

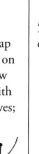

4 Press the long edges of the handles ¼" to the wrong side. Press again in half so the pressed edges meet. Stitch.

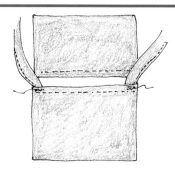

Place the ends of the handle ½" to the inside of the top of the front/back with the flap seams and stitch.

5 Iron on the initial if you have not embroidered one.

American Girl doll

Zippered Cable Sweater and Double-Knit Pants

Zippered Cable Sweater

(designed by Ceci Riehl)

Supplies:
50 gm fingering weight or baby yarn (Lanett, Dale Baby Ull)
16" or 24" circular needle** size US 3 or size needed to obtain gauge
Crochet hook or second small needle for binding off
Stitch markers (optional)
Cable needle
5" separating zipper
Hand-sewing needle with matching thread

**This sweater is worked back and forth on one 16" or 24" circular needle, which will serve also as stitch holder; however, a longer or shorter circular needle may be used.

Gauge: 2" = 12 or 13 sts.

Pattern stitches:
L4: Ladder (over 4 sts). Repeat these 4 rows:
Rows 1 and 4: K4.
Rows 2 and 3: P4.
(On the outside, change the st. On the inside, knit the knits or purl the purls*.)

C6: Braided cable (over 6 sts). Repeat these 4 rows:
Row 1: Put first 2 sts on cable needle in front of work. K2, K2 from cable needle, K2.

Götz doll

Row 2 and 4 (inside rows): P6.
Row 3: K2 put next 2 sts on cable needle in back of work, K2, K2 from cable needle.

Body:
Cast on 132 (front: 34 X 2; back: 64).
Row 1: K1 P1 K1 K4 P4 *(K2, P2) repeat from * to last 13 sts K2 P4 K4 - K1 P1 K1.
Row 2: K1 P1 K1 P4 K4 *(P2, K2) repeat from * to last 13 sts P2 K4 P4 - K1 P1 K1.
Repeat these two rows once more.

Pattern:
Row 1: K1 P1 K1 - K4 L4 K2 P2 C6, place marker, *(P2, K2) repeat from * 21 times, P2, place marker, C6 P2 K2 L4 K4 - K1 P1 K1.
Row 2: On the inside, knit the knits and purl the purls* except for the first and last 3 sts of every row. These sts are always K1 P1 K1. This creates a seed st facing that will be turned under and won't show when zipper is set in.
Repeat rows 1 and 2 until work measures 3¼".
Begin shaping armholes and neck edge.

Right front:
Keep working in established pattern throughout this section.
Starting with an outside row, work across 34 sts. Place marker (it should fall

between 2 purl sts). Turn.
Continue in established pattern on just these 34 sts until center front matches length of zipper teeth (5"). End with inside row.
Next (outside) row: Bind off 3 sts. Continue across.
Next (inside) row: Work 23 sts. Turn. You will have 8 sts on right needle. S1 K1 PSSO continue across. Work 7 more rows, decreasing 1 st at beginning of each outside row (neck edge). End with an outside row at armhole (19 sts left). Cut yarn, leaving a 24" tail.

Back:
Attach yarn at bottom of armhole split. Work across next 64 sts in 2 X 2 rib. Place marker (again between 2 purl sts). Turn. Work across these 64 sts in rib pattern until back is same length as front at armhole. Cut yarn, leaving a 24" tail.

Left front:
Reattach yarn at base of other armhole. Work left front until it is the same length as right—or until the same number of "rungs" have been worked in the "ladder" section.

Shaping:
Beginning with outside row, bind off 3 sts. Work to armhole.
Next row: Work 21 st K2 tog. Turn. Continue working 7 more rows in pattern decreasing 1 st at end of each outside row. End with an outside row, finishing at armhole edge (19 sts).
Bind off and join shoulders. Place last loop back on needle with backstitches. Transfer 8 sts from center front to other end of needle. There will be a gap where the neck shaping sts are. This will be dealt with later.
Transfer 8 sts from right center front and 19 sts from right shoulder to other end of needle. Bind off and join right shoulder sts as for left. Put last loop on needle with back stitches. Cut yarn.

Collar:
You should have 8 center front sts on each end of the needle, 26 back sts, and two loops from the shoulder bind offs.
Attach yarn at right center front edge (beginning of outside row). Knit 8 sts.

Pick up and knit 10 sts from neck edge. Knit the extra loop from the shoulder bind off together with the first loop of the back sts. Work across back in rib, continuing pattern from back. Knit the last of the back sts and the second bind off loop together. Pick up and knit 10 sts from left neck edge. Knit 8 sts from left front (62 sts). (You need a multiple of 4 plus 2 sts for the collar to work out right.) Work all these sts in 2 X 2 rib beginning with P2 for 1¾". This should work out so the rib pattern from the back continues through the collar and the 2 X 2 rib continues to the front of the collar. The first and last sts on the outside will be knit. (These sts will be on the underside of the collar when it is turned down.) Bind off loosely in rib. Cut end leaving 6" to weave in.

Sleeves:
Cast on 42 sts.
Row 1: *(P2 K2) repeat from * 10 times, P2.
Row 2: *(K2 P2) repeat from * 10 times P2 (knit the purls and purl the knits). Repeat these two rows once more.
Pattern row: *(P2 K2) repeat from * 4 times, P2, C6, P2, *(K2,P2) repeat from * 4 times.
Inside row: Knit the purls and purl the knits.
Repeat these two rows until sleeve is 4¾" long. Bind off all sts.

Finishing:
Sew sleeves into armholes. Sew sleeve seams. Weave in loose ends.
To insert the zipper in center front, open and separate the zipper. Place one half under each center front edge so that the bottom edge of the zipper is flush with the bottom edge of the sweater. Using a sewing needle and matching thread, stitch the zipper to the sweater. Fold the excess zipper tape at the top edge down on the wrong side. Tack in place and cut off the excess, if necessary.

Double-Knit Pants

Supplies:
⅓ yd. black double-knit fabric
5" elastic (¼" wide)

1 Cut two fronts, two backs, and one waistband from the knit fabric.

2 With right sides together, sew the side seams of each pant leg. Press seam allowances open. Press the hem edges of the pants ½" to the wrong side and stitch.

3 Sew the center front and center back seams with right sides together.

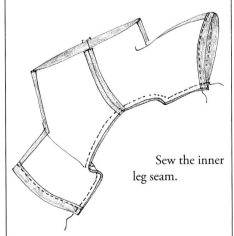

Sew the inner leg seam.

4 With right sides together, pin the short ends of the waistband together, forming a circle. Stitch and press the seam allowances open.

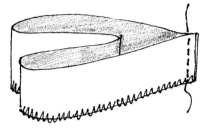

5 Serge or zigzag stitch along one long edge of the waistband.

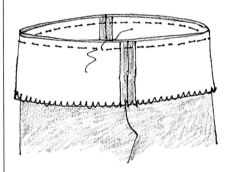

Sew the right side of the unstitched edge to the right side of the top edge of the pants, matching the waistband seam to the center back seam of the pants.

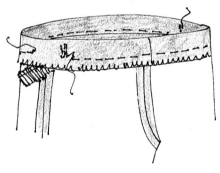

6 Fold the waistband over into the inside of the garment so the waistband is ½" wide. Pin carefully and topstitch from the right side, leaving a 1" opening at each side seam to insert elastic.

7 Thread the elastic through the back waistband and secure it at each side seam with a few machine stitches. Stitch the openings closed.

Another pair of dolls wanted to participate in the fun at the mall, too. They are shopping at the same store wearing more stylish, casual clothes. The first doll, who loves glitter and jewels, is wearing a baseball-type of jacket with "princess" embroidery, a t-shirt with mesh sleeves, another pair of low-rise jeans, and a heart belt. The jacket, made from glitter denim and pink twill, zips up the front with a metal separating zipper. A plastic zipper could also be used. The embroidery motif on the front is stitched before the fabric is cut out. The t-shirt has long bell sleeves made from mesh knit fabric with a repeating heart pattern. Her shirt is decorated with a jeweled heart. The jeans are the same low-rise jeans as the jeans with the inset. The inset was eliminated and more jeweled hearts decorate the pant legs. The cute little belt is made from craft foam cut in heart shapes and linked together on a ribbon. These hearts were cut from foam, but pre-cut shapes could also be used.

Her shopping partner wears a pretty knitted sweater with a lacy look at the hem and sleeve edges, embroidered khaki jeans, and a fringed shoulder bag. This sweater, knit on a circular needle, ties at the neck for easy dressing. Her bag with fringe and eyelets is made from faux suede, such as Ultrasuede. It uses a suede strip for the handle, and has suede fringe that is sold by the yard. Five metal eyelets decorate the front of the bag. For a bright colorful look, try making the bag from colored suede or leather-look fabrics and multi-colored eyelets instead. The embroidered jeans are the same pair worn with the varsity jacket in the School Fashions section.

From left to right: Götz and American Girl dolls

Shop 'Til You Drop, Part II

Princess Jacket, T-Shirt with Mesh Sleeves, Low-Rise Flared Jeans and Heart Belt

Götz doll

Princess Jacket

Supplies:

¼ yd. glitter denim fabric

¼ yd. pink twill for the sleeves

5" separating zipper

3" x 22" pink ribbing

Optional: Princess embroidery design from *Doll Clothing Designs* by Joan Hinds from Cactus Punch, 2 colors 40 wt. embroidery thread, and stabilizer

1 Before cutting jacket fronts, trace the left front jacket onto a piece of the denim fabric large enough to fit in your hoop. Following your machine's instructions, embroider the design where indicated on the pattern piece with the embroidery thread. Cut the left jacket front out and tear away the stabilizer.

2 Cut out the right front, one back, and two waistline ribbing attachments from the denim fabric. Cut two sleeves from the pink twill. Cut a piece of ribbing 3" x 11" for the waistline, another piece 1½" x 8" for the collar, and two pieces 1¼" x 3½" for the cuffs.

3 With right sides together, sew the fronts to the back at the shoulders. Press the seam allowances open.

4 Zigzag stitch or serge the center front edges.

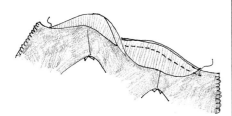

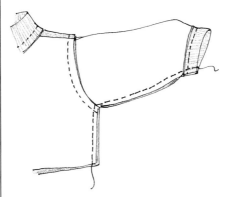

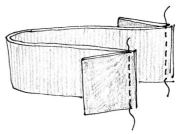

7 Gather the sleeve caps slightly to fit the armholes. Stitch the sleeves to the armholes with right sides together.

Turn to the right side and press. Fold the ribbing in half lengthwise and stitch the short ends to the cut ends of the ribbing attachments.

5 Fold the collar in half lengthwise with wrong sides together. Pin the folded collar around the neckline of the jacket between the center-front fold lines with right sides together. The collar should taper with the cut ends of the collar included in the seam allowance (see illustration above). Fold the center fronts over the collar along the fold lines with right sides together and pin at the neckline edge. Stitch the collar to the neckline.

8 Sew the underarm seam from the wrist to the waist with right sides together.

9 Turn the center front edges toward the inside of the garment along the fold line indicated on the pattern piece. Press.

With right sides together, sew the ribbing and attachments to the bottom of the jacket. Serge or zigzag the seam allowances to finish.

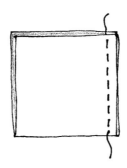

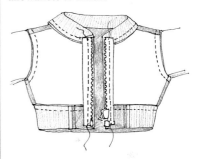

6 Fold the cuff ribbing in half lengthwise with wrong sides together. Stretch the cuffs to fit the lower edge of each sleeve and zigzag stitch or serge.

Fold the waistline ribbing attachments in half with right sides together and stitch along one of the short ends.

10 Sew the zipper to the front opening of the jacket. The top and bottom of the zipper should be flush with the top and bottom edges of the jacket.

T-Shirt with Mesh Sleeves

Supplies:
¼ yd. t-shirt knit fabric
¼ yd. mesh knit fabric
2" Velcro strip
Iron-on jeweled heart

1 Cut one front and two backs from the t-shirt knit fabric. Cut two sleeves from the mesh fabric.

2 With right sides together, sew the center back seam to the dot marked on the pattern piece. Serge or zigzag stitch each side of the back seam separately, including the unstitched part of the seam. Press the seam allowances open and topstitch the open area of the seam.

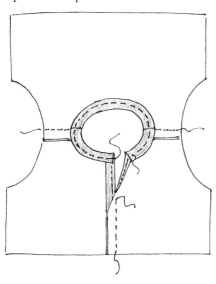

3 With right sides together, sew the shoulder seams together. Press the neckline edge ¼" to the wrong side and stitch.

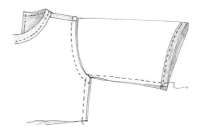

4 Press the lower edges of the sleeves ¼" to the wrong side and stitch. Sew the sleeve caps to the armholes, easing the sleeves as necessary. Stitch the underarm seams, starting at the sleeve hem and finishing at the lower edge of the shirt.

5 Serge or zigzag stitch the lower edge of the shirt, press the edge ⅜" to the wrong side, and topstitch.

6 Lapping right over left, sew the Velcro to the back opening.

Gölz doll

TIP

For decorations for t-shirts and jeans, don't overlook the scrapbook department in craft stores! They will often feature many tiny motifs with jewels or appliqué that will stick on the pages. If you are sure that you will not be washing your doll's clothing, you can safely use these motifs by just pressing them on the fabric.

Low-Rise Flared Jeans

Supplies:
⅓ yd. lightweight denim fabric
1¾" Velcro strip
6 iron-on jeweled hearts (¾")

1 Cut two fronts, two backs, and one belt loop from the fabric.

2 With right sides together, sew the center front seam. Sew the center back seam to the dot marked on the pattern piece. Press the seam allowances open and topstitch around the open area of the seam.

3 Sew the side seams with right sides together. Serge or zigzag stitch the lower edges of the pants and press ½" to the wrong side. Stitch ⅜" from the fold.

4 Serge or zigzag stitch the top edge of the pants and press ½" to the wrong side. Stitch ⅜" from the fold.

5 Press the long edges of the belt loop ¼" to the wrong side and stitch close to each folded edge. Cut in half widthwise. Press each raw end ¼" to the wrong side.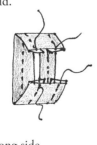

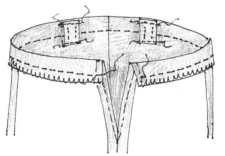

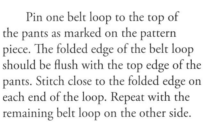

Pin one belt loop to the top of the pants as marked on the pattern piece. The folded edge of the belt loop should be flush with the top edge of the pants. Stitch close to the folded edge on each end of the loop. Repeat with the remaining belt loop on the other side.

6 Sew the loop side of the Velcro to the left center-back opening. One long side should be placed a scant ⅛" under the edge of the opening. Sew the hook side of the Velcro to the other back opening with the entire piece of Velcro stitched on the wrong side of the back opening. When the pants are closed, the back opening edges will meet, but not overlap.

7 Iron on the hearts on the pant legs, using the photograph as a guide.

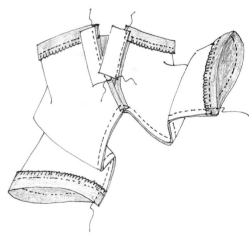

8 With right sides together, sew the inner leg seam.

Heart Belt

Supplies:
Sheet of craft foam (2mm thick)
⅔ yd. ribbon (⅛" wide)
Craft glue

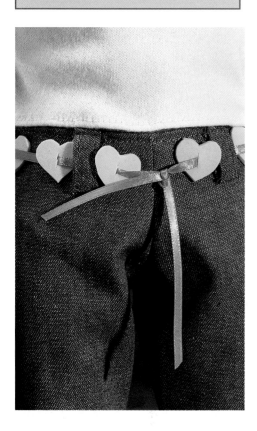

1 Cut 10 hearts from the foam. Cut slits in the center of the foam heart so that the ribbon can be woven through.

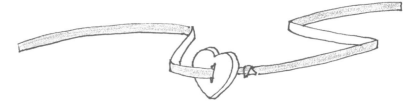

2 Find the center of the ribbon. Measure 1" from the center to the right and tie a knot. Slide a heart on the ribbon to the knot. Measure ⅞" away and tie another knot. Slide a heart on the ribbon to the knot. Repeat until you have 5 hearts on the belt. Glue the hearts to the ribbon so they will lie flat.

3 Measure 1" from the left of the center of the ribbon and repeat Step 2. Tie the belt onto the waist of the jeans through the belt loops.

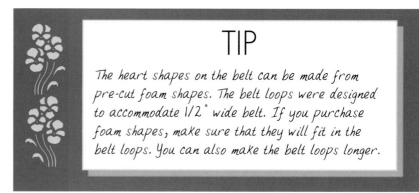

TIP

The heart shapes on the belt can be made from pre-cut foam shapes. The belt loops were designed to accommodate 1/2" wide belt. If you purchase foam shapes, make sure that they will fit in the belt loops. You can also make the belt loops longer.

Lacy Long-Sleeved Sweater, Embroidered Khaki Pants and Fringed Bag with Eyelets

American Girl doll

Lacy Long-Sleeved Sweater

(designed by Ceci Riehl)

Supplies:
50 gm fingering weight, baby yarn or sock yarn (Lanett, Dale Baby Ull)
16" or 24" circular needle size US 3 or size needed to obtain gauge
Small crochet hook

Gauge: 2" = 12 or 13 sts. This sweater is worked back and forth on one 24" circular needle, which will serve also as st holder.

Pattern stitches:
K2tog—Knit 2 sts together as one (1 st decreased).
Sk2po—Slip 1 st; knit 2 together, pass slipped st over last one on needle (2 sts decreased).
Ssk—Slip two sts as if to knit; knit both together through the back loops (1 st decreased).

Yo—Pass yarn over needle as if to knit (1 st added, which will create a hole).
Psso—Pass slipped st over last st on needle and drop.

Body:
Cast on 93 sts. Knit 1 row.
Work rows 1-11 of lace pattern.
Lace pattern:
Row 1: K1, k2tog, *k3, yo, k1, yo, k3, sk2po; rep. from * to last 10 st, k3, yo, k1, yo, k3, ssk, k1.
Row 2 and all even rows: purl.
Row 3: K1, k2tog, *k2, yo, k3, yo, k2, sk2po; rep from * to last 10 sts, k2, yo, k3, yo, k2, ssk, k1.
Row 5: K1, k2tog; *k1, yo, k5, yo, k1, sk2po; rep from * to last 10 sts, k1, yo, k5, yo, k1, ssk, k1.
Row 7: K1, k2tog; *yo, k1, k2tog, yo, k1, yo, ssk, k1, yo, sk2po; rep from * to

last 10 sts, yo, k1, k2tog, yo (k1, yo, ssk) twice, k1.
Row 9: K3, *(k2tog, yo) twice, k1, yo, ssk, k3; rep from *
Row 11: K4 *k2tog, yo, k1, yo, ssk, k5; rep, from * to last 9 st, k2tog, yo, k1, yo, ssk, k4.
Continue working in stockinette st until piece measures 3" from one of the points in hem. End with a purl row.

Back: You will work just the back stitches now, leaving the front stitches on the needle.
Beginning with outside (knit) row knit 46 (half-way across). Turn. Bind off 4 sts purl across.
Next row: Bind off 4 sts. Knit across to last 2 st before bind-off, ssk (37 sts). Turn. Purl next row.

Next row: S1 k1 psso, knit across to last 2, ssk.

Repeat these last two rows until 29 sts remain in this section.

Continue in stockinette st until piece measures 6" from a hem point for long sleeved sweater.

Cut yarn leaving an 18" tail.

Left Front:

Join yarn at armhole (where turns were made). Bind off 4 sts; knit 43.

Next row: Bind off 5 sts; purl across (38 sts remain in the front section). Work as for the back, decreasing 1 st each edge on knit rows until 30 sts remain.

Beginning with an outside (knit) row knit 15. Turn. Work these 15 sts in stockinette st until piece measures 5½".

Next rows: K11, W & T. P11. K10, W & T. P10. K9, W & T. P9. K8, W & T. P8, K7, W & T. P7.

Bind off and join these 7 sts with 7 sts from the back. Knit across 8 sts remaining of left front. Cut yarn leaving a tail.

Right Front:

Transfer the **15** sts of the right front to the other needle. Attach yarn at edge. Work these 15 sts in stockinette st until the right side is as long as the left at center front, ending with a knit row.

Next rows: P11, W & T. K11. P10, W & T. K10. P9, W & T. K9. P8, W & T. K8, P7, W & T. K7.

Bind off and join these 7 sts with 7 sts from back. Do not cut yarn. Knit across 8 remaining sts of right front. Now you have 8 sts from left front, 1 loop, 15 center back sts 1 loop, and 8 right front stitches on the needle (33 sts).

Finishing neck edge:

Knit across 33 sts.

Next row: p1 *(yo, p2tog) repeat from * across.

Next row: Knit.

Bind off all sts. Do not cut yarn.

Neckline tie strings:

With small crochet hook inserted into last loop, work 2 or 3 single crochet sts along neck edge to bring the yarn to the first row of the neck edging. Work chain sts until the string measures 5". Pull end through. Cut end and weave back into tie. Attach yarn at other side of opening across from the first tie and make another chain for the second tie.

Sleeves:

Cast on 43 sts.

Knit one row.

Work rows 1-8 of lace pattern.

Row 9: K1, k2tog, *(k2tog, yo) twice, k1, yo, ssk, k3; rep from * to last 3 st, ssk, k1.

Rows 10 and 12: Purl.

Row 11: K3 *k2tog, yo, k1, yo, ssk, k5; rep, from * to last 9 st, k2tog, yo, k1, yo, ssk, k3 (41 st).

Rows 13 and 15: K1, k2tog, knit across to last 3 st, ssk, k1 (37 st).

Continue in stockinette st until piece measures 3½" from beginning, measuring from one of the points in the hem.

Begin shaping top of sleeve:

Bind off 3 sts at beginning of next 2 rows.

Decrease row: s1, k1, psso, knit across to last 2 sts ssk. Purl across all the inside rows.

Continue to decrease one st each edge of every knit row, until 13 sts remain. Sleeve should measure 5½" to 6" long.

Bind off all sts.

Finishing:

Sew left side seam. Set in sleeves. Sew sleeve seams. Weave in loose ends. Press to block being careful not to exceed the heat tolerated by your yarn. Test on a gauge swatch if you are uncertain.

Khaki Embroidered Flared Jeans

The instructions for these jeans are included with the Varsity Jacket in the School Fashions section on page 44.

Fringed Bag with Eyelets

Supplies:
6" x 9" piece of suede-like fabric, such as Ultrasuede
½" x 15" piece of suede for handle
4" faux suede fringed trim
5 eyelets (³⁄₁₆")
Eyelet tool

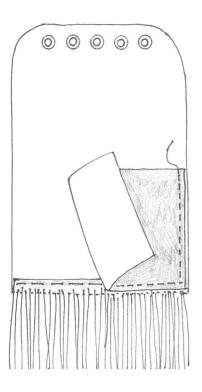

1 Cut one front bag and one back bag with flap from the fabric.

2 Place the trim along the wrong side of the lower edge of the back bag with flap. Cut off any excess trim on the sides. Baste. Place the front bag over the trimmed edge of the back bag with flap so that the lower edges are flush. Stitch around the sides and lower edge of the bags with a ⅛" seam allowance.

3 Stitch each end of the suede handle inside the top edges of the side seams.

4 Using the eyelet tool, place the eyelets in the flap, as marked on the pattern piece. Fold the flap over to the front of the bag.

School Fashions

These dolls look smart in their fashionable school attire! The gray wool and plaid cotton skirts with box pleats in the front and back are sewn from the same pattern. The doll with the gray skirt has paired it with a white shirt and sweater vest. The shirt has princess seams and three-quarter length sleeves with cuffs that are split in the middle with a "notch." The sweater vest is quick and easy since it is made from a woman's sock! You can find many patterns in socks to match any outfit. This cranberry sock with flecks is a perfect complement to the gray skirt.

The next doll wears the cotton plaid skirt, paired with a cable-knit pullover sweater. The sweater, knitted on a circular needle, is a heather gray-green and red color that picks up the colors of the plaid in the skirt. It closes with three buttons at one of the shoulder seams.

Varsity jackets are always seen at school. The last doll wears a soft plum-colored jacket with embroidered khaki jeans. The jacket is made from cotton flannel with matching suede-look fabric sleeves instead of the traditional wool and leather. Other fabric choices could be any medium-weight soft fabric and faux leather or suede for the sleeves. This jacket has coordinating colors, but try contrasting colors for a traditional look. Doll-sized snaps and an embroidered name add a realistic touch to the front of the jacket. The jeans are made from a khaki twill fabric that was embroidered before it was cut. Look for small embroidery designs for doll clothing, especially designs that can be separated into parts, so the whole design does not have to be used.

Götz doll

Wool Pleated Skirt, White Button-Front Shirt
and Sweater Vest Made from Socks

Wool Pleated Skirt

1 Cut one front, one back, and one waistband from the wool fabric.

2 With right sides together, stitch the short sides of the front and back together and press. Serge or zigzag stitch the hem edge of the skirt. Press ⅜" to the wrong side and stitch.

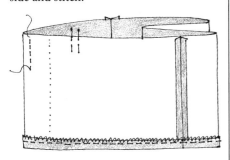

3 Find the center of the top edge of the skirt and mark 1" away with a pin. With another pin, make a mark 1¼" from the first. Bring those two points, with right sides together, to make a vertical fold.

Stitch down 1" from the top edge. Repeat with the other side of the front skirt. Press the folds to make box pleats.

4 Repeat Step 3 with the back of the skirt.

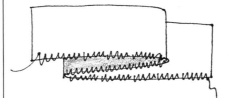

5 Serge or zigzag stitch along one long edge of the waistband. With right sides together, sew the short ends. Press the seam allowances open.

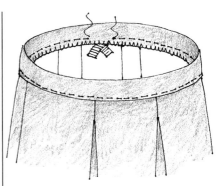

Pin the waistband to the top of the skirt with right sides together. The seam of the waistband should be placed at the center back. Fold the waistband over to the inside of the skirt so the waistband is ½" wide. Topstitch in place, leaving a 1" opening at the back. Thread the elastic through the casing and secure the ends. Topstitch the opening closed.

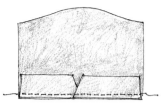

3 Fold the collar in half lengthwise with right sides together. Stitch across the short ends. Clip the corners, turn right-side out, and press.

4 With right sides together, center the collar along the neckline of the shirt. The collar does not go all the way to the center front edges. Stitch.

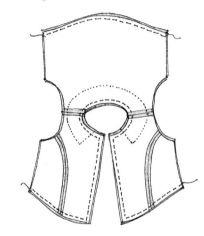

5 With right sides together, pin the lining to the shirt, sandwiching the collar in between. Sew around the neckline, down the center fronts, and around the hemline in both front and back. Clip the curves, turn right-side out, and press. Baste the lining to the shirt around the armholes.

6 Sew two cuffs with right sides together along the angled end and the shorter side. Repeat with the remaining cuffs to make a total of four. Place two cuffs together with the angled ends at the center. Overlap them so that the cut edges fit the bottom of the sleeves. The cuffs will look as if a "notch" is cut in the center. Stitch. Finish the seams and press the seam allowances toward the sleeves.

7 With right sides together, stitch the sleeve caps to the armholes, easing as necessary. Sew the underarm seam from the cuff to the hem of the shirt.

8 Sew the buttons to the right front opening as marked on the pattern piece. Sew snaps underneath the buttons on the right front. Sew the other snap halves to the left front opening.

Götz doll

White Button-Front Shirt

Supplies:
¼ yd. white light-weight fabric, such as broadcloth or cotton sateen
4 buttons (¼")
4 small snaps

1 Cut four fronts, four side fronts, two backs, one collar, two sleeves, and eight cuffs from the fabric.

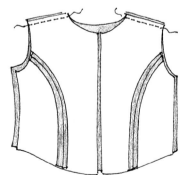

2 Sew the side fronts to the fronts with right sides together. With right sides together, stitch two fronts to one back at the shoulder seams. Repeat with the other set for the lining. Press seam allowances open.

Sweater Vest Made from Socks

(designed by Marilee Sagat)

Supplies:

1 pair women's patterned trouser socks
2½" Velcro strip, cut in half lengthwise

Make sure that the socks are not anklets and that the pattern goes entirely around the foot portion of the sock. In evaluating socks for this sweater, make sure that the pattern on the sock is not directional, because the sweater will be using the sock ribbing as the hem of the sweater.

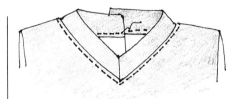

1 Cut out the front and back pieces of the sweater, centering the pattern pieces on the sock with the bottom of the pattern piece aligned with the sock cuff. Cut open the side fold of the sweater front and cut open both folds of the sweater back.

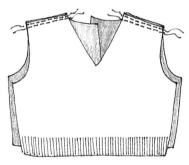

2 Cut out two pieces of binding 1¼" x 5½" from the foot portion of the sock for the armholes. Cut another piece 1¼" x the full width of the sock for the neck binding. Sew the shoulder seams with right sides together at ¼" and ⅛". Trim any excess fabric close to ⅛" stitching line.

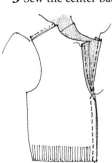

3 Sew the center back seam from the hem edge to the dot indicated on the pattern piece. Fold the remaining back edges of the sweater ¼" to the wrong side and top stitch along this edge.

4 For the neck binding, fold the binding in half lengthwise and again in half along the width. At the double folded point, sew at a 45-degree angle starting at the double fold stitching to the raw edges. This creates a v-shape in the binding. Trim the seam to ⅛".

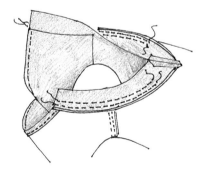

5 Fold each short edge of the binding ¼" to the wrong side. Place the stitched center of the binding to the center front of the neckline of the sweater and pin. The binding should be lying on the top of the sweater. Using a ¼" seam, attach the binding to the sweater starting at one back edge, slightly stretching the binding to fit the neck opening. Stop stitching to within ½" of the point in the front of the sweater. Start from the other back edge and stop ½" from the point in the front. Stitch both seams again ⅛".

6 Flip the binding up so that the seam is laying flat against the sweater body. Topstitch the entire neck edge, including the point, very close to the binding seam, making sure that you are catching the binding/sweater seam. This method will make sure that the binding stays standing straight up and won't fall forward.

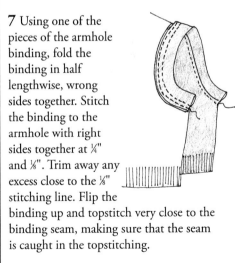

7 Using one of the pieces of the armhole binding, fold the binding in half lengthwise, wrong sides together. Stitch the binding to the armhole with right sides together at ¼" and ⅛". Trim away any excess close to the ⅛" stitching line. Flip the binding up and topstitch very close to the binding seam, making sure that the seam is caught in the topstitching.

8 Sew the side seam from the hem to the armhole binding at ¼" and ⅛", trimming excess fabric.

9 Lapping right over left, sew the Velcro to the back opening.

Pleated Skirt and Cable-Knit Pullover Sweater

Pleated Skirt

Use the same patterns and instructions for the pleated skirt on page 37 using a medium-weight cotton plaid fabric.

Cable-Knit Pullover Sweater

(designed by Ceci Riehl)

This sweater is worked back and forth on one circular needle, which will also serve as a stitch holder. The length of the circular needle isn't important. If a 16" or 24" needle is not comfortable, it is possible to use a longer or shorter needle for this sweater.

American Girl doll

Supplies:

50 gm fingering weight or baby yarn (Lanett, Dale Baby Ull.)
16" or 24" circular needle, size US 3 or size needed to obtain gauge
16" or 24" circular needle, size US 1 or smaller than first needle
Crochet hook or second small needle for binding off
Stitch markers (optional)
Cable needle
3 buttons (⅜")

Gauge: 2" = 12 or 13 sts.

Abbreviations:
T2KCF—Transfer 2 k sts to cable needle; hold in front of work.
K2FC—K2 from cable needle
T2PCB—Transfer 2 p sts to cable needle; hold in back of work.
P2FC— P2 from cable needle
T2KCB—Transfer 2 k sts to cable needle; hold in back.
Pm—Place a st marker on the needle.

Cable pattern #1:
(Over 12 sts) Repeat these 12 rows:
Row 1: T2KCF, P2, K2FC, K4, T2PCB, K2, P2FC
Rows 2, 4 and 6: K2, P8, K2
Row 3: P2, T2KCF, K2, K2FC, T2KCB, K2, K2FC, P2
Row 5: P2, K2, T2KCB, K2, K2FC, K2, P2
Row 7: T2PCB, K2, P2FC, K4, T2KCF, P2, K2FC
Rows 8, 10, 12: P2, K2, P4, K2, P2
Row 9: K2, P2, K4, P2, K2
Row 11: K2, P2, T2KCB, K2, K2FC, P2, K2

Cable pattern #2:
Braided cable (over 6 sts) Repeat these 4 rows:
Row 1: T2KCF, K2, K2FC, K2
Row 2 and 4 (inside rows): P6
Row 3: K2, T2KCB, K2, K2FC

Sleeves:
With the smaller needle, cast on 36 sts. Work 4 rows in k1, p1 rib, increasing 4 sts evenly spaced across 4th row (40 sts). Change to larger needle.
K15; pm, p2, k6, p2, pm, k15.
All inside rows: Knit the knits and purl the purls.
Work all sts between marker and end of needles in stockinette st. Between markers work p2, braided cable, p2.
Increase one st at each edge of a knit row every 6 rows until you have 44 sts. Continue until sleeve is 5" long. Bind off all sts.

Body:

C.O. 118 sts.

With smaller needle work 4 rows in k2, p2 rib.

Next row: *(k2, p2) repeat from * 7 times, m1*, k2, m1, *(p2, k2) repeat from * across (120 st).

Change to larger needle.

Next row: Knit the knits and purl the purls*. Purl the 2 added (m1) stitches. These two new stitches will be in the center of the center front cable.

(NOTE: The cable sts are worked on the front of the sweater (60 st). The back is plain stockinette. The cable sts are arranged as follows: the cable pattern #1 is in the center front, with braided cables on either side, separated by a column of 2 knit sts. Two purl sts are worked before and after each cable OR like this: K10, marker, p2, braided cable, p2, marker, k2, p2 (cable pattern #1) p2; k2, marker, p2, braided cable, p2, marker, k10, k60.)

First row: K10, pm, p2, k6, p2, pm, k2, p2 (k2,p2,k4,p2,k2) p2, k2, pm, p2, k6, p2, pm, k70.

Next row: Knit the knits and purl the purls.

Now, beginning with row 1 of both cable patterns, work braided cable patterns between markers; keep p2, k2, p2 columns between cable patterns; work cable pattern #2 on center 12 sts. (You will repeat the braided cable 3 times for each completion of cable pattern 1.) Continue until sweater measures 3" from start. End with a knit row. Note the number of the pattern row just finished for cable patterns. #1_____, #2_____.

Divide front and back.

Next row: P 60, Turn. K60. Work these 60 sts in stockinette until piece measures 6".

Cut the yarn.

Tie the yarn on at armhole in center of work. Work across to outer edge. Continue working front, beginning with the next rows of cable patterns. Work until front measures 5". End with an inside row.

Shaping neck:

Next row: Work across 24 st W&T. Work back to left armhole edge. Keep pattern as established on these shoulder sts.

Next row: Work 23 sts W & T. Work back to armhole. Work 22 sts W&T. Work back to the armhole. Continue in this manner turning one stitch before previous turn, until 18 sts remain. Beginning with next outside row, work these 18 sts in k1, p1 rib.

Next row: Work in rib back to left edge.

Next row: (k1, p1, k1, p1, yo, s1, p1, psso) repeat twice more (three buttonholes made). Work 2 more rows in

k1, p1 rib. Bind off 18 sts Cut yarn. Attach yarn at first st on front after the bound off sts. Work across in pattern to right armhole. Turn. Work 24 sts in pattern. W&T. Work to armhole. Again, keeping pattern as established, work 23 sts W& T. Work back to armhole. Work 22 sts W& T. Work back to the edge. Repeat these last two rows 4 more times. End at right armhole edge (18 sts). Bind off and join these 18 sts with 18 from back. It may be helpful to place a marker after the 18th st or mark this st with a pin or bit of yarn, because it is hard to see the wrapped sts. Do not cut yarn.

Work 24 sts from back. Work remaining 18 sts in k1, p1 rib. Work 2 more rows of rib on these 18 sts. Bind off these 18 sts. Do not cut the yarn.

Neck edge:

Transfer last loop to smaller needle. Pick up and knit 2 sts along edge of ribbed flap. Work across in k1, p1 rib. Work 3 sts in edge of buttonhole flap. Work 2 more rows in rib. Bind off all sts. Cut yarn.

Finishing:

Sew left side seam up 3" from hem. Set in sleeves. Sew underarm sleeve seams. Weave in loose ends. Sew three small buttons on back shoulder rib section below buttonholes.

Varsity Jacket and Khaki Embroidered Flared Jeans

American Girl doll

Varsity Jacket

Supplies:

¼ yd. wool or cotton flannel
¼ yd. suede-look fabric for sleeves
3" x 22" ribbing
5 decorative snaps (⁵⁄₁₆")*
Snap setter tool
40 wt. embroidery thread
Tear-away stabilizer

*Used in this project:
 Dritz for Dolls

1 Cut one back and two fronts from the flannel. If you plan to machine embroider a name on the right front, do so before you cut it out, using the placement on the pattern piece as a guide. Following the instructions for your embroidery machine, use the 40 wt thread and stabilizer.

2 Cut the sleeves from the suede fabric. Cut a piece of ribbing 2½" x 13" for the waistline, another piece 1½" x 8" for the collar, and two pieces 1¼" x 3½" for the cuffs.

3 With right sides together, sew the fronts to the back at the shoulders. Press the seam allowances open.

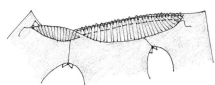

4 Zigzag stitch or serge the center front edges.

5 Fold the collar in half lengthwise with wrong sides together. Pin the folded collar around the neckline of the jacket between the center-front fold lines, with right sides together. The collar should taper with the cut ends of the collar included in the seam allowance (see illustration above). Fold the center fronts over the collar along the fold lines with right sides together and pin at the neckline edge. Stitch the collar to the neckline. Turn the center front edges toward the inside of the garment along the fold line indicated on the pattern piece. Press. Baste the hem edge of the folded center front to the jacket at the seam line.

6 Fold the cuff ribbing in half lengthwise with wrong sides together. Stretch the cuffs to fit the lower edge of each sleeve and zigzag stitch or serge.

7 Gather the sleeve caps slightly to fit the armholes. Stitch the sleeves to the armholes with right sides together.

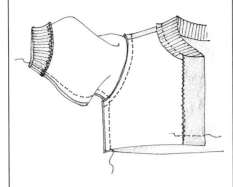

8 Sew the underarm seam from the wrist to the waist with right sides together.

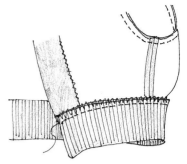

9 Fold the waistline ribbing in half lengthwise with right sides together. Stitch the short ends and turn right-side out. Pin to the bottom edge of the jacket, stretching the ribbing to fit. Zigzag stitch or serge. Press the ribbing down away from the jacket.

10 Using the snap setter tool, apply the snaps to the front opening. Apply one snap in the waistline ribbing and one approximately ¼" below the neckline. Space the rest of the snaps at 1" intervals.

TIP

You can also make the Varsity Jacket into a letter jacket, if you prefer. Using school colors, make the body of the jacket from wool, and the sleeves can actually be cut from leather. The ribbing usually matches the body color. If you choose to use leather, you will need to use a leather needle and a fabric glue stick to hold the leather in place while stitching. This will be easier on your hands and eliminate pinholes.

Khaki Embroidered Flared Jeans

Supplies:
⅓ yd. khaki twill fabric
5" elastic (¼" wide)
Optional: Butterfly and Flowers embroidery design from *Doll Clothing Designs* by Joan Hinds for Cactus Punch (size is 1½" x 1½"), 5 colors of 40 wt. embroidery thread, and tear-away stabilizer.

1 Before cutting the pants, trace the right and left front pants pieces onto the fabric. On the left front pants, embroider the complete design where indicated on the pattern piece with the embroidery thread. On the right front pants, embroider only the butterfly with the embroidery thread. Cut out both pants pieces.

2 Cut two backs and one waistband from the fabric.

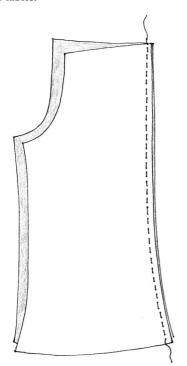

3 With right sides together, sew the side seams of each pant leg. Press seam allowances open. Press the hem edges of the pants ½" to the wrong side and stitch.

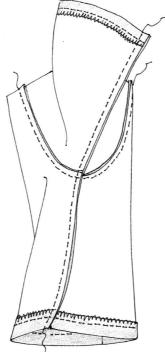

4 Sew the center front and center back seams with right sides together. Sew the inner leg seam.

5 With right sides together, pin the short ends of the waistband together, forming a circle. Stitch and press the seam allowances open.

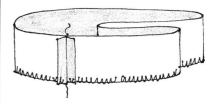

6 Serge or zigzag stitch along one long edge of the waistband. Sew the right side of the unstitched edge to the right side of the top edge of the pants, matching the waistband seam to center back seam of the pants.

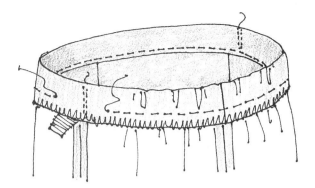

7 Fold the waistband over into the inside of the garment so the waistband is ½" wide. Pin carefully and topstitch from the right side, leaving a 1" opening at each side seam to insert elastic.

8 Thread the elastic through the back waistband and secure it at each side seam with a few machine stitches. Stitch the openings closed.

Summer Picnic

From left to right: Götz, Tolly Girl, and American Girl dolls

Everyone loves to spend a lazy summer day at a picnic. The dolls shown here are cooking up a feast in their colorful picnic attire. One of the dolls wears a simple denim dress with a ruffle at the hemline. The decoration is made from felt butterflies on one shoulder and on the lower front of the dress. The antennae are stitched with a machine embroidery thread using a reinforced straight stitch. This decorative stitch is programmed in many sewing machines. It is a straight stitch that goes back and forth over each stitch twice to give it a hand stitched look. If your machine doesn't have this capability, stitch the antennae by hand, or sew over the stitching from beginning to end twice. Her bag is coordinated to match the butterflies in the dress and closes with a small piece of Velcro.

The next doll is wearing a ruffled collar shirt and matching twill skirt with a ruffle and an elastic waist. The flared sleeve cuffs are another fashion trend that dolls want to be a part of. The fabric for the shirt and skirt ruffle is a rayon-polyester blend to give the shirt and ruffle a very soft, drapey look. Cotton prints can be used, but the flared cuffs and ruffles may look too stiff. The neckline is finished with a self-bias strip over the ruffle. Making a miter at the center front of the bias creates a v-shape to the neckline.

The last doll wears a soft mauve short-sleeved version of the other lacy sweater shown with the embroidered khaki pants on page 31. Changes to the instructions for the short sleeves are given here, also. The sweater is worn with bright white straight-leg capri pants. The pants have an elastic waist and a button sewn to the cuffs at the bottom of the pants.

Don't forget their sandals! These easy instructions can help you can make custom sandals for any outfit you choose. The pair shown with the denim dress is made from denim trimmed with three colors of ribbon to match the outfit colors. The other pair is made with striped elastic, but any solid color will work. The soles are cut from both thick and thin craft foam sheets. The soles are layered and glued together. Be sure the glue you use is suitable for craft foam. Pre-cut foam shapes decorate the tops. Look for other non-fraying materials such as leather, Ultrasuede, or ribbon to make the sandal uppers. Trim the uppers with beads, buttons, or bows!

Denim Dress with Butterfly Trim, Shoulder Bag and Sandals

Götz doll

Denim Dress with Butterfly Trim

Supplies:

½ yd. light-weight denim or chambray fabric

Scrap of matching lightweight cotton fabric for lining

4" x 2" pieces each of pink, yellow, and lime green felt

Pink and yellow 40 wt. decorative embroidery thread

4" Velcro strip

Fabric glue

1 Cut one front, two backs, and one ruffle 1¾" x 40" from the denim fabric. Cut one front facing and two back facings from the cotton fabric.

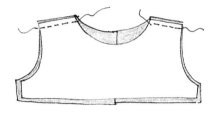

2 Finish the lower edges of the lining pieces by serging or with a zigzag stitch. With right sides together, sew the shoulder seams of the front and backs and press open. Repeat with the lining pieces.

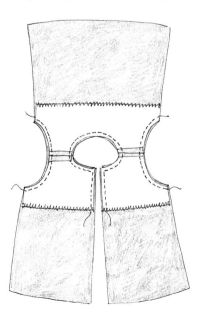

3 With right sides together, sew the lining to the dress around the neckline, the armholes, and down the center backs just as far as the length of the lining pieces. Clip the curves; turn to the right side and press.

4 Sew the backs along the center back seam to the dot marked on the pattern piece. Press the seam allowances open, including the unstitched part of the seam. Topstitch around the opening up to the neckline including the dress/lining seam.

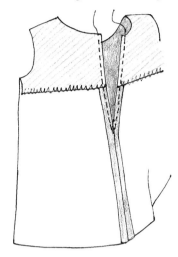

5 With right sides together, sew the side seams.

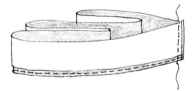

6 Narrow hem one long edge of the ruffle. Sew the short ends with right sides together.

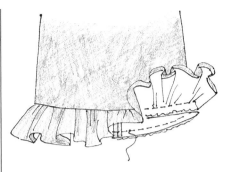

Gather the other long edge to fit the bottom of the dress. Stitch. Finish the seam by serging or with a zigzag stitch.

7 Cut butterflies from the felt: one yellow, one green, and two pink. Cut butterfly bodies from the felt: one pink, one green, and two yellow. Attach the butterflies to the dress as marked on the pattern piece by stitching down the center of each body. Sew the antennae with the decorative thread using a reinforced straight stitch. (This stitch makes each stitch twice.) If you do not have this stitch on your machine, sew each antenna twice. Glue the butterfly bodies to the center of the butterflies with the fabric glue.

8 Lapping right over left, sew the Velcro to the back opening.

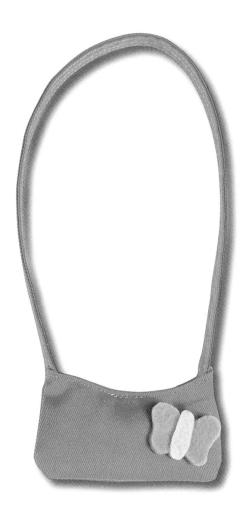

Shoulder Bag

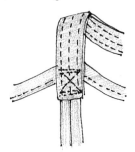

Supplies:
5" x 16" piece of twill fabric
Scraps of yellow and lime green felt
½" x ¾" piece of Velcro
Fabric glue

1 Cut two handbags and one strap from the twill fabric. Cut one butterfly from the green felt and one butterfly body from the yellow felt.

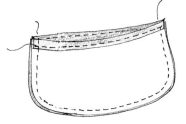

2 Press the top edge of each handbag ¼" to the wrong side and stitch close to the edge. With right sides together, stitch the handbags around the curved outside edge. Clip the curves, turn to the right side and press.

3 Press the long edges of the handle ¼" to the wrong side. Press the handle in half lengthwise so that the folded edges meet. Stitch close to the folded edges, down the middle, and along the other side.

Pin the ends of the handle inside the handbag and stitch.

4 Glue the butterfly body over the butterfly. Glue the butterfly to the handbag where marked on the pattern piece.

Götz doll

Sandals

Supplies:

4" x 5" piece of lightweight denim fabric

9" each of pink and lime green ribbon (¼" wide), cut in half

9" of yellow ribbon (⅛" wide), cut in half

Clear invisible thread

4" x 5" lime green craft foam (³⁄₁₆" thick)

4" x 5" white craft foam (2mm thick)

Glue, such as Aleene's Clear Gel Tacky Glue, or Crafter's Pick: The Ultimate

Temporary adhesive spray

Craft knife, such as an Exact-o knife, or hot knife, such as Creative Versa-tool

1 Cut two uppers from the denim fabric. Press both long sides of each upper ¼" to the wrong side and stitch.

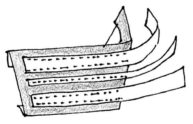

2 Spray the wrong side of the green ribbon with the temporary adhesive. Place it a scant ⅛" from the shorter long side and stitch along both sides with the clear thread. Do the same with the pink ribbon and stitch it a scant ⅛" from the longer side. Stitch the yellow ribbon down the center of the upper between the other two ribbons.

3 Cut two soles from both the white and green foam. Cut the thinner foam with a scissors. Cut the thicker foam with the craft or hot knife, following the manufacturer's instructions.

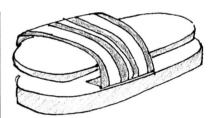

4 Glue the ends of the right side of the uppers to the thick foam as seen in the illustration. Hold the uppers to the sole tightly until the glue dries. Glue the thin foam over the thick foam, covering the denim upper edges. Again, hold tightly until the glue dries.

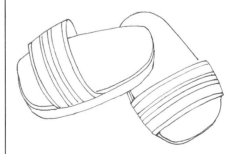

Six-Gore Skirt with Ruffle and Ruffled Collar Shirt

Tally Girl doll

Supplies:
⅓ yd. print fabric
¼ yd. solid twill fabric
3" Velcro strip
12" satin ribbon (⅛" wide)
4½" elastic (¼" wide)

Ruffled Collar Shirt

1 Cut one front, two backs, two sleeves, two cuffs, two collars, and one bias strip 1¼" x 9¾" from the print fabric.

2 With right sides together, sew the shoulder seams. Press seam allowances open.

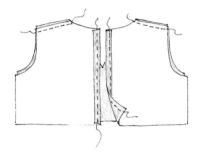

3 Serge or zigzag stitch the center back edges and press ¼" to the wrong side. Stitch.

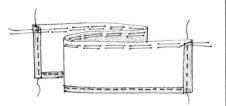

4 Narrow hem one long edge of each collar. Press the short ends ¼" to the

wrong side and stitch. Gather the unstitched edge of the collar and pin to the shirt neckline. The collars should meet at center front and extend to the center back edges. Baste.

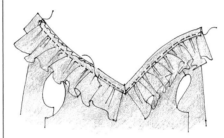

5 Press one long edge of the bias strip ¼" to the wrong side. With the right side of the bias and the wrong side of the shirt neckline together, stitch the bias to the neckline edge, extending the short ends of the bias ¼" beyond the center backs. Fold the bias over to the right side and stitch close to the folded edge, tucking in the short ends. Miter the center front of the bias by taking a few hand stitches to make a v-shape in the bias.

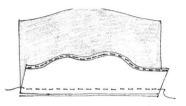

6 Narrow hem the lower edges of the sleeve cuffs. With right sides together, sew the cuffs to the lower sleeve edges.

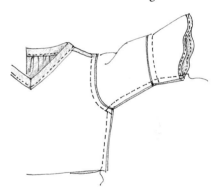

Sew the sleeve caps to the armholes, easing to fit. Sew the underarm seam from the sleeve edges to the hem of the shirt, with right sides together.

7 Press the hem edge of the shirt ¼" to the wrong side. Press another ¼" and stitch.

8 Lapping right over left, sew the Velcro to the back opening.

9 Tie a bow with the ribbon and tack to the bias at the center front.

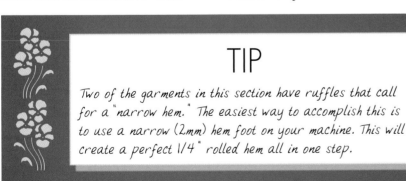

TIP

Two of the garments in this section have ruffles that call for a "narrow hem." The easiest way to accomplish this is to use a narrow (2mm) hem foot on your machine. This will create a perfect 1/4" rolled hem all in one step.

Six-Gore Skirt with Ruffle

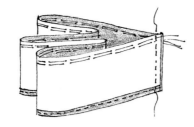

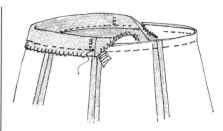

1 Cut one front, two side fronts, one back, two side backs, and one waistband from the twill fabric. Cut one ruffle 2¼" x 40" from the print fabric.

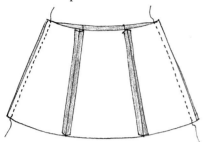

2 With right sides together, sew the side fronts to each side of the front skirt. Sew the side backs to each side of the back skirt. Sew the side seams with right sides together.

3 Narrow hem one long edge of the ruffle. Sew the short ends with right sides together. Gather the unstitched edge of the ruffle to fit the bottom of the skirt.

Stitch it to the skirt with right sides together. Finish the seam allowances by serging or with a zigzag stitch.

4 Sew the short ends of the waistband with right sides together. Press one long edge of the waistband ¼" to the wrong side. With the right side of the waistband to the wrong side of the skirt, sew the unpressed edge of the waistband to the skirt's top edge. Fold the waistband over the skirt and stitch close to the folded edge, leaving 1" openings at each side seam. Thread the elastic through the back waistband and stitch the elastic at the side seams. Stitch the openings closed.

American Girl doll

Lacy Short-Sleeved Sweater

(designed by Ceci Riehl)

Follow the instructions for the Lacy Long-Sleeved Sweater on page 31 with the following exceptions:

The back sweater length should measure 5½".

The front sweater length should measure 5".

Sleeves:
Cast on 33 sts.
Knit one row.
Work rows 1-8 of lace pattern.
Row 9: K1, k2tog, *(k2tog, yo) twice, k1, yo, ssk, k3; rep from * to last 3 st, ssk, k1.

Rows 10 and 12: Purl.
Row 11: K3 *k2tog, yo, k1, yo, ssk, k5; rep, from * to last 9 st, k2tog, yo, k1, yo, ssk, k3 (31 sts).
Skip rows 13 and 15 and begin shaping the top of the sleeve. The short sleeve should measure about 3½" long.

Lacy Short-Sleeved Sweater, Straight-Leg Capri Pants and Flower Sandals

Straight-Leg Capri Pants

Supplies:
⅓ yd. twill fabric
4½" elastic (¼" wide)
2 buttons (⅜")

1 Cut two front pants, two back pants, one waistband, and two cuffs from the fabric.

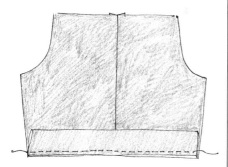

2 With right sides together, sew the side seams of each pant leg. Press seam allowances open. Fold the cuffs in half lengthwise with wrong sides together and press. Stitch the cut edges of the cuffs to the lower edges of the pants with right sides together.

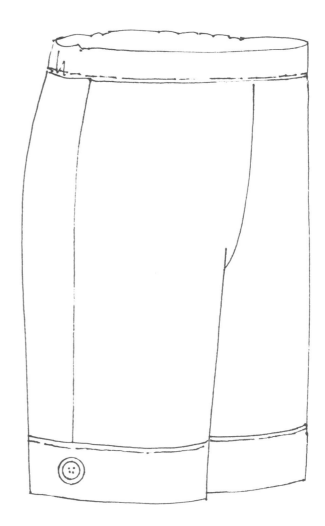

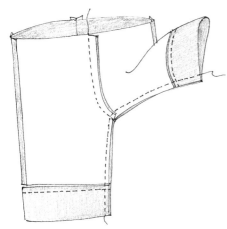

3 Sew the center front and center back seams with right sides together. Sew the inner leg seam.

4 With right sides together, pin the short ends of the waistband together, forming a circle. Stitch and press the seam allowances open.

5 Serge or zigzag stitch along one long edge of the waistband. Sew the right side of the unstitched edge to the right side of the top edge of the pants, matching the waistband seam to center back seam of the pants.

6 Fold the waistband over into the inside of the garment so the waistband is ½" wide. Pin carefully and topstitch from the right side, leaving a 1" opening at each side seam to insert elastic.

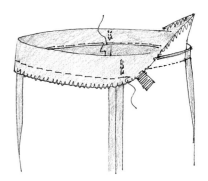

7 Thread the elastic through the back waistband and secure it at each side seam with a few machine stitches. Stitch the openings closed.

8 Sew a button to each cuff approximately ½" from the side seam.

Flower Sandals

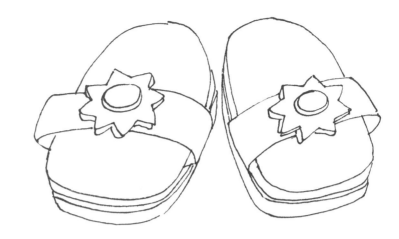

1 Cut two soles from each of the foam pieces with a craft scissors.

2 Cut the elastic in half. Fold the ends of the elastic ¼" over one of the pieces of foam where marked on the pattern piece and glue.

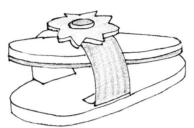

3 When dry, glue the remaining two colors of foam together. Glue the top layer with the elastic attached over them.

4 Glue the flowers to the top of the elastic in the center. Glue the dots to the center of each flower.

The dolls are enjoying a bright sunny day on the playground. They love riding scooters, rollerblading, and skateboarding, so they need appropriate attire for these activities. The rollerblader wears a knit t-shirt and shorts. The shirt closes at the shoulders with Velcro instead of at the back to give the sewer another style of t-shirt to add to her doll's wardrobe. The shorts are embroidered on the back with the word "princess." Shorts with words and phrases are very popular with girls today.

The denim capri pants worn by the doll with the scooter have eyelets tied with leather lacing at the lower side seams. Eyelets and lacing are also a big fashion trend in clothing for girls. The pants are paired with a peasant shirt made from a cotton print fabric and lace edging. The neckline and sleeves have a casing made from bias tape and elastic to ensure a good fit. A macramé necklace made from hemp and colorful beads is just the right fashion accessory. Her visor is cut from a sheet of thin craft foam and decorated with pre-cut foam shapes. You can apply other decorative shapes, such as hearts or stars to create several different styles. Of course, when the dolls actually start playing, they will wear their helmets!

From left to right: Götz and American Girl dolls

Wheelin' Around

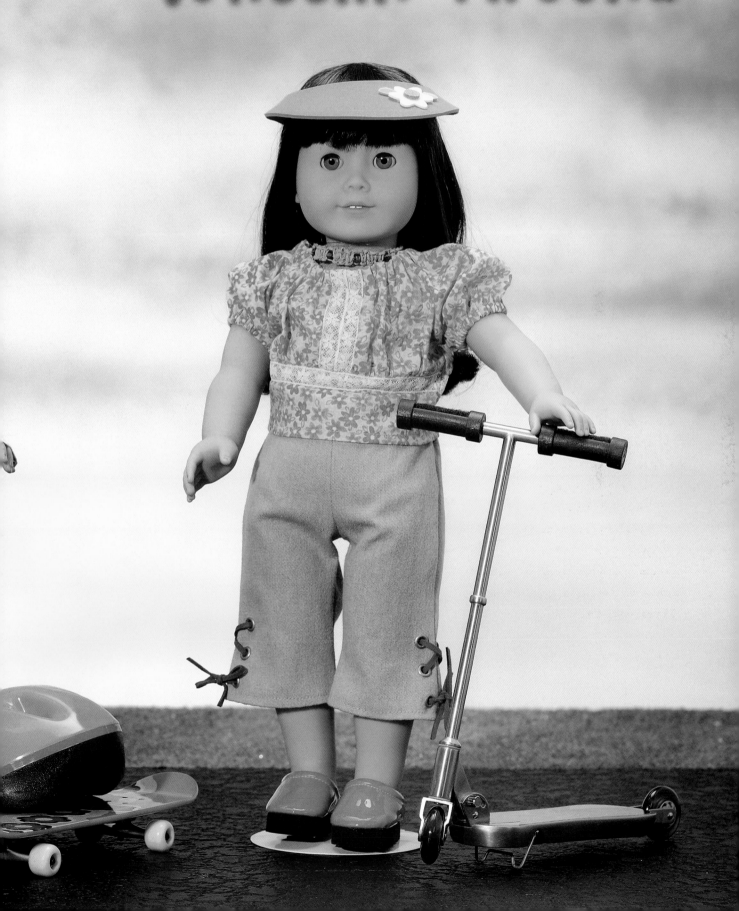

Shorts and T-Shirt

Supplies:
- ¼ yd. print knit fabric
- ¼ yd. solid color knit fabric
- 1½" Velcro strip, cut in half lengthwise
- 11" elastic (1/4" wide)
- Optional: Princess embroidery design from *Doll Clothing Designs* by Joan Hinds for Cactus Punch, 40 wt. embroidery thread in 1 color, stabilizer, and temporary adhesive spray

T-Shirt

1 Cut one front, one back, and two sleeves from the print fabric. From the solid fabric, cut two binding strips 1¼" x 7" for the sleeves, and a 1¼" x 10" strip for the neckline.

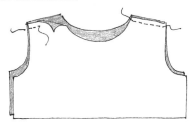

2 Sew the left shoulder seam with right sides together. Sew the right shoulder seam only ⅜" from the armhole edge.

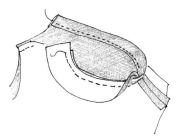

3 Press one long edge of the binding ¼" to the wrong side. Beginning and ending at the right shoulder seam edges, pin the right side of the binding to the wrong side of the neckline, turning each end

under ¼". Stitch. Fold the binding over to the right side and stitch close to the pressed edge.

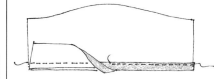

4 Press one long edge of the sleeve bindings to the wrong side. With the right side of the binding to the wrong side of the lower sleeve edge, sew the binding to the sleeve. Fold the binding over to the right side and stitch close to the pressed edge.

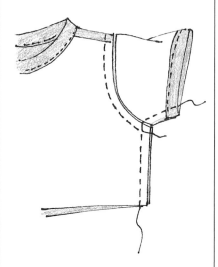

5 With right sides together, sew the sleeve caps into the armholes, easing as necessary. Sew the underarm seam from the sleeve edges to the hem of the shirt.

Götz doll

6 Press the hem of the shirt 3/8" to the wrong side. Stitch.

7 Sew the hook part of the Velcro to the back shoulder opening (no need to finish the seam allowance first). Turn the front seam allowance ¼" to the wrong side and stitch the loop side of the Velcro to the underside of this edge.

Shots

1 Cut four shorts from the solid color fabric.

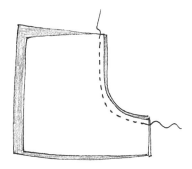

2 With right sides together, stitch the center front and back seams.

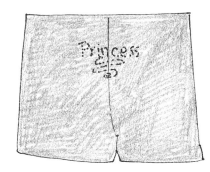

3 If embroidering on the back of the shorts, put stabilizer into the embroidery hoop. Spray the hoop with the temporary adhesive spray. Center the back of the shorts on the stabilizer. The embroidery design is centered over the back seam 1" above the curve of the crotch in the shorts. Stitch only the word "Princess" on the shorts, increasing the design by 20 percent. Trim away all excess stabilizer as close to the design as possible.

4 Stitch the side seams with right sides together.

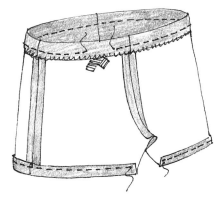

5 Serge or zigzag stitch the top edge of the shorts. Press this edge ½" to the wrong side. Top stitch ⅜" from the pressed edge, leaving a 1" opening at the center back for casing. Thread elastic through the casing and stitch the ends together, overlapping slightly. Stitch the opening closed.

6 Serge or zigzag stitch the hem edges of the shorts. Press this edge ¼" to the wrong side and topstitch.

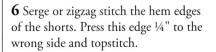

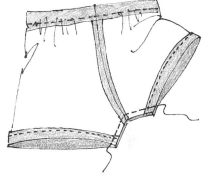

7 With right sides together, sew the inner leg seam.

TIP

Sometimes stitching with a sewing machine near the edge of the knit fabrics can cause stretching of the fabric, especially along the hemline. To avoid stretching, reduce the pressure on your machine's presser foot.

Peasant Top, Capri Pants with Lacing, Sun Visor and Macramé Necklace

Peasant Top

Supplies:
¼ yd. cotton print fabric
⅔ yd. white lace insertion
3" Velcro strip
½ yd. single-fold bias tape
10½" elastic (¼" wide)
8" elastic (⅛" wide)

1 Cut one upper front, two upper backs, one lower front, two lower backs, and two sleeves from the fabric.

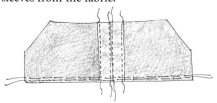

2 Cut two pieces of the lace 3½" long. Place them side-by-side on the center front of the upper front and zigzag stitch them to the fabric. Cut off any excess at the top and bottom.

3 Gather the lower edges of the upper front and upper backs. Stitch the upper front to the lower front and the upper backs to the lower backs.

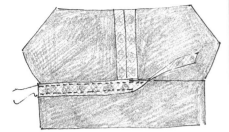

4 Place the lace below the seam on the lower front. Zigzag stitch on both sides of the lace. Sew the lace to each lower back below the seam in the same manner.

5 With right sides together, sew the sleeves to the front and backs.

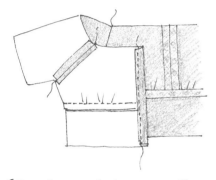

6 Press the center back openings ¼" to the wrong side. Press again and stitch.

7 To make a casing for the neckline, place bias tape over the neckline with right sides together and stitch. Fold the tape to the inside, tucking in the short ends, but not stitching them, and stitch close to the folded edge of the bias tape.

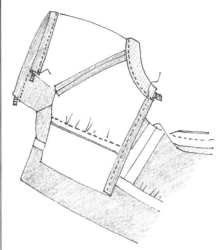

8 Thread the wider elastic through the casing and secure the ends with a few stitches.

9 Press the edge of each sleeve ¼" to the wrong side. Press another ¼" and stitch close to the fold. Cut the narrower elastic in half. Thread a piece of elastic through each casing and secure at the ends.

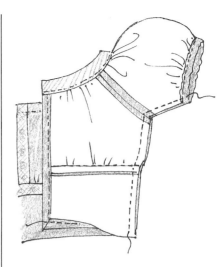

10 With right sides together, sew the underarm seams.

11 Press the hem of the top ¼" to the wrong side. Press another ¼" again and stitch.

12 Lapping right over left, sew the Velcro to the back opening.

TIP

The lace on the Peasant Top is called lace insertion. That means it has straight edges on both sides of the lace. You can substitute lace edging, which means that the lace has one straight side and one side that is scalloped. If you choose to use lace edging, be sure to put the straight sides together on the center front. The same lace edging can also be used below the front and back seams. The straight side should be stitched next to the seam line.

Capri Pants with Lacing

Supplies:
⅓ yd. light-weight denim fabric
4½" elastic (¼" wide)
12 eyelets (³⁄₁₆")
Eyelet tool
1 yd. leather lacing (⅛" wide)

1 Cut two front pants, two back pants, and one waistband from the fabric.

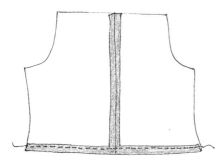

2 With right sides together, sew the side seams of each pant leg. Press seam allowances open. Press the hem edges of the pants ½" to the wrong side and stitch.

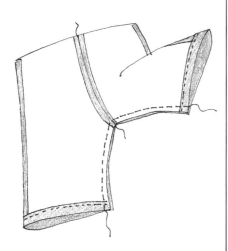

3 Sew the center front and center back seams with right sides together. Sew the inner leg seam.

4 With right sides together, pin the short ends of the waistband together, forming a circle. Stitch and press the seam allowances open.

5 Serge or zigzag stitch along one long edge of the waistband. Sew the right side of the unstitched edge to the right side of the top edge of the pants, matching the waistband seam to center back seam of the pants.

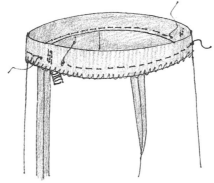

6 Fold the waistband over into the inside of the garment so the waistband is ½" wide. Pin carefully and topstitch from the right side, leaving a 1" opening at each side seam to insert elastic.

7 Thread the elastic through the back waistband and secure it at each side seam with a few machine stitches. Stitch the openings closed.

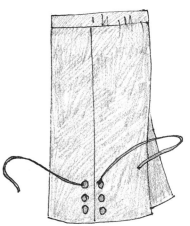

8 Using the eyelet tool, insert the eyelets where indicated on the pattern pieces. Cut the lacing in half and thread each piece through the eyelets, tying them at the bottom two eyelets.

Sun Visor

Supplies:

7" x 8" piece of craft foam (2mm)

1 pre-cut craft foam flower shape (1⅛" wide)

1 green pre-cut craft foam flower shape (1⅛" wide)

1 pre-cut craft foam dot (⅜" wide)

Glue, such as Aleene's Clear Gel Tacky Glue, or Crafter's Pick: The Ultimate

1 Cut the visor from the craft foam.

2 Cut two petals from the green flower to use as leaves. Glue the flower to the visor as marked on the pattern piece. Glue the dot to the center of the flower. Glue the "leaves" on each side of the flower.

3 Overlap the ends of the visor at an angle and glue together.

Macramé Necklace

Supplies:

1 skein hemp cord
9 beads (4mm)

1 Cut one length of hemp cord 33" long. Cut two more pieces 16" long.

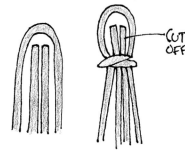

2 Fold the longer piece in half. Tie this piece to the other two lengths making a knot with a loop. (The loop should be large enough to fit a bead tightly.) Cut the top of the two shorter lengths above the knot.

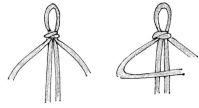

3 Making sure that the shorter hemp lengths are in the center, take the left side of the longer length and place it in the middle. Take the right side and place it over the left side so that it resembles a "4."

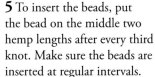

4 While holding the right side, put it under the middle hemp lengths, through the "4" and pull up to the knot. Do these same steps, only start the "4" on the right side. Switch every other knot from right to left and back.

5 To insert the beads, put the bead on the middle two hemp lengths after every third knot. Make sure the beads are inserted at regular intervals.

6 The necklace should measure about 8" long. To end the necklace, tie a bead at the end to use as a clasp and knot at least twice.

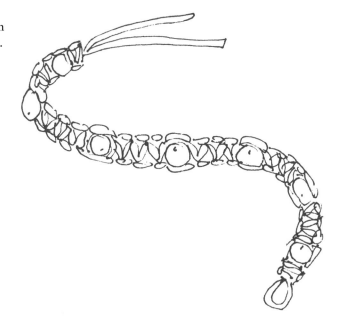

She shoots, she scores! These dolls have lots of fun playing soccer and basketball. The soccer uniform is made from a mesh knit for the top and a crinkle nylon fabric for the shorts. The shirt pulls over the head with no back opening. The opening is large enough to go over most dolls' heads. Red and white are popular colors, but you can make the uniform in the colors of your doll's favorite team. All uniforms have numbers. The shirt has an embroidered number in the front and a large one that irons on in the back.

A warm-up suit is necessary for time spent on or off the bench. The jacket and pants are made of fleece and trimmed with braid. The pants have flared legs just like the warm-up suits seen in girls' ready-to-wear departments. The separating zipper gives the jacket a realistic touch.

Basketball is a popular sport for girls today. Dolls want their own uniforms, too. The fabric is a mesh knit, with the same type of fabric for the trim. The sleeveless shirt goes over the head just like the soccer uniform. The trim on the side is edged with middy braid. Applying it with a fusible tape makes it easy to sew. The large numbers on the shirt front and back are ironed on, but the smaller one on the shorts is machine embroidered.

From left to right: Laura Ashley, American Girl, and Götz dolls

Playing Hard

Soccer Uniform

Shirt

1 Cut one front, one back, and two sleeves from the mesh fabric. Cut the ribbing into four equal pieces, each measuring 6½".

2 If you choose to embroider your shirt with a number, place the shirt front over stabilizer in the hoop with the temporary spray adhesive. Embroider the number on the front as marked on the pattern piece with contrasting thread. Cut away the stabilizer.

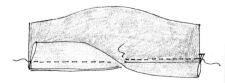

3 Fold two of the strips in half lengthwise with wrong sides together. Pin each strip to the right side of the bottom of each

sleeve and stitch. Press the ribbing trim down. Topstitch with matching thread on the shirt ⅛" from the binding seam.

4 Apply a folded strip around the back neckline in the same manner, clipping the curves in the seam allowances. Topstitch on the shirt ⅛" from the binding seam.

5 For the front v-shaped neckline, fold the remaining strip first lengthwise with wrong sides together. Fold again crosswise to mark the center front. Make a mitered 45-degree corner and stitch. Trim the seam to ⅛".

Pin to the right side of the neckline and stitch, starting at the shoulder and ending 1/2" from the point. Repeat for the other side of the front neckline.

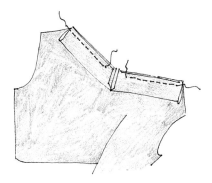

Flip the trim up and topstitch ⅛" from the seam on the shirt. This topstitching will secure the point of the binding to the shirt.

6 With right sides together, sew the front to the back at the shoulder seams.

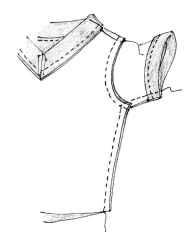

7 Stitch a row of gathering stitches to the top of each sleeve cap. Pull up the gathers

slightly to fit the armhole. Stitch. Sew the underarm seam with right sides together from the sleeve edge to the bottom of the shirt.

8 Hem the shirt by pressing the lower edge ¼" to the wrong side and stitch.

9 Iron on the number to the center of the back of the shirt.

Shorts

1 Cut two fronts and two backs.

2 With right sides together, sew the side seams from the waist to the dot marked on the pattern piece. Press the entire seam allowance open for each seam. Top stitch around the side slit.

3 If you choose to embroider your shorts with a number, place the left side of the shorts over stabilizer in the hoop with the temporary spray adhesive. Embroider the number on the front with contrasting thread. Cut away the stabilizer.

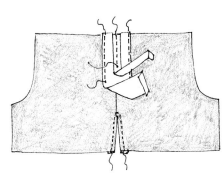

4 Place the narrow braid trim over the center of the twill tape or ribbon and stitch. Press one end of the twill tape/ braid combination ¼" to the wrong side. Pin the tape over the side seams, with the pressed edge of the tape placed at the dot. Stitch. Repeat with the other side. Cut any excess at the waistline of the shorts on each piece.

5 Press the lower edges of the shorts ¼" to the wrong side. Press another ¼" and stitch.

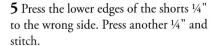

6 Finish the top edge of the shorts by serging or zigzag stitching. Press this edge ⅝" to the wrong side and stitch ½" from the pressed edge, leaving an opening at the center back to insert elastic. Thread the elastic through the opening and secure the ends. Stitch the opening closed.

Warm-Up Suit

Supplies:
⅓ yd. dark color fleece fabric
¼ yd. light color fleece fabric
11" elastic (¼" wide)
2 yd. white braid trim (⅜" wide)
6" separating zipper

American Girl doll

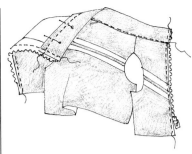

Jacket

1 Cut two upper fronts, one upper back, two sleeves, and one collar from the lighter fabric. Cut two lower fronts and one lower back from the darker fabric.

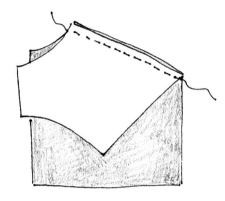

2 With right sides together, sew the upper fronts to the lower fronts and the upper back to the lower back.

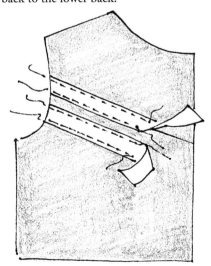

Cut a piece of trim to fit over the seam line. Place the lower side of the trim on the seam line and stitch along both sides. Place another piece of trim ¼"

below the seam line and stitch along both sides of the trim. Repeat with the other front side and the back.

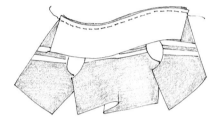

3 Stitch the fronts to the back at the shoulder seams with right sides together. Sew one long edge of the collar to the neck edge of the jacket with right sides together. Serge or zigzag stitch the other long edge of the collar.

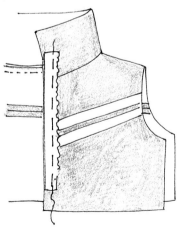

4 Place the wrong side of half of the zipper along the front opening. The bottom of the zipper should be placed ¾" from the lower edge of the jacket. (The zipper will only extend up approximately one half of the collar width. If the zipper fabric extends beyond one half of the width of the collar, trim off the excess.) Baste the zipper ¼" from the front edge.

Open out the zipper to the right side and pin ¼" from the stitched seam, folding the collar to the inside over the zipper and covering the jacket/collar seam. Stitch, using a zipper foot or an edge-stitching presser foot. Repeat with the other side of the jacket and the other half of the zipper.

5 Pin the serged edge of the collar over the jacket/collar seam line and stitch in the ditch to secure.

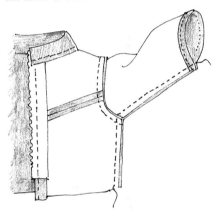

6 Fold the lower sleeve edges ½" to the wrong side and stitch. With right sides together, sew the sleeve caps to the armholes. Sew the underarm seams from the sleeve edge to the lower edge of the jacket.

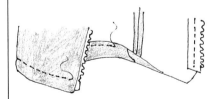

7 Serge the lower edge of the jacket and pin this edge ½" to the wrong side. Stitch ⅜" from the folded edge.

Pants

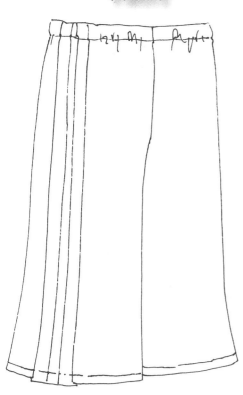

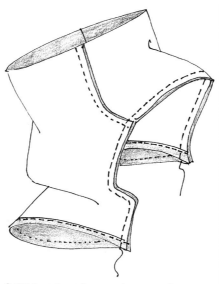

3 With right sides together, sew the center front and center back seams. Stitch the inner leg seam with right sides together.

4 Serge or zigzag stitch the top of the pants. Fold the seam ½" to the wrong side and stitch ⅜" from the fold, leaving a 1" opening at the center back to insert the elastic into the casing.

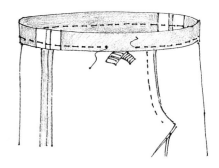

5 Insert the elastic into the casing. Overlap the ends and stitch. Stitch the opening closed.

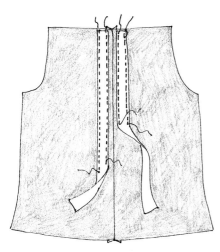

1 Cut four pants from the darker fabric. With right sides together, sew two pants together at the side seam. Place the trim ¼" to the right of the side seam and stitch along both sides of the trim. Place another piece ¼" to the left of the side seam and stitch along both sides. Repeat with the remaining pants pieces.

2 Fold the lower edge of each pant leg ½" to the wrong side and stitch.

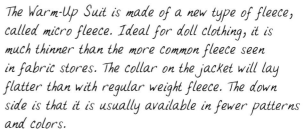

TIPS

The Warm-Up Suit is made of a new type of fleece, called micro fleece. Ideal for doll clothing, it is much thinner than the more common fleece seen in fabric stores. The collar on the jacket will lay flatter than with regular weight fleece. The down side is that it is usually available in fewer patterns and colors.

Sewing a zipper in fleece fabric means that the zipper is exposed. The stitching lines are approximately 1/4" from the zipper and should look as straight as possible. Most sewing machines have a foot with a metal edge on one side that is called an edge stitching foot. You can then adjust the needle position so that the metal edge will follow the edge of your fabric. If your machine has this foot, it will help keep your stitching line straight.

Götz doll

Basketball Uniform

Supplies:
¼ yd. athletic mesh knit fabric
⅛ yd. athletic mesh knit fabric in a contrasting color for the trim
1 yd. middy braid (¼" wide)
Fusible tape (¼" wide)
11" elastic (¼" wide)
2 felt iron-on numbers (2" wide)
Optional: Embroidered number (¾" wide) program in sewing machine, 40 wt. embroidery thread in two colors for number on front of shirt and shorts, stabilizer, and temporary spray adhesive

Shirt

1 Cut one front and one back from the mesh fabric. From the contrasting fabric, cut one strip 1¼" x 6½" for the front neckline edge. Cut another strip 1¼" x 5½" for the back neckline edge. Cut two strips 1¼" x 8¼" for the armhole edges.

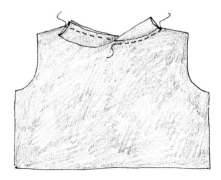

2 Fold the back neckline trim in half with wrong sides together. Pin to the right side of the neckline and stitch. Open up the seam and press. Topstitch on the shirt with contrasting thread, ⅛" from the trim/shirt seam.

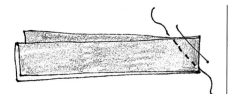

3 For the front v-shaped neckline, fold the front neckline trim first lengthwise with wrong sides together. Fold again crosswise to mark the center front. Make a mitered 45-degree corner and stitch. Trim the seam to ⅛".

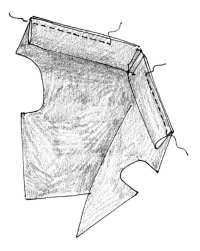

Pin to the right side of the neckline and stitch, starting at the shoulder and ending ½" from the point. Repeat for the other side of the front neckline.

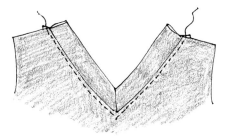

Flip the trim up and topstitch with contrasting thread ⅛" from the seam on the shirt. This topstitching will secure the point of the binding to the shirt.

4 With right sides together, sew the back to the front at the shoulders.

5 Fold the sleeve trims in half lengthwise with wrong sides together. Pin to the right side of the armholes and stitch. Open up

the seam and topstitch with contrasting thread on the shirt ⅛" from the trim/armhole seam. Sew the underarm seam from the armhole to the bottom of the shirt.

6 Finish the shirt's bottom edge by serging or with a zigzag stitch. Press this edge ½" to the wrong side. Stitch ⅜" from the pressed edge.

7 Apply the iron-on numbers to the shirt front ½" from the bottom of the seam line at the "v", and the number in the center of the back 1" below the neckline seam.

Shorts

1 Cut two fronts and two backs. Cut two strips from the contrasting fabric 1" x 8½" for the side of the shorts. Cut two more strips 1¼" x 10" for the trim at the bottom of the shorts.

2 With right sides together, sew the side seams of the shorts all the way to the bottom edge.

3 If you choose to embroider your shorts with a number, place the left side of the shorts over stabilizer in the hoop with the temporary spray adhesive. Embroider the number on the front as marked on the pattern piece with contrasting thread. Cut away the stabilizer.

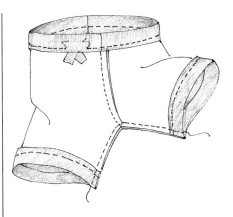

4 Cut two pieces of middy braid 8½" long. Place the fusible tape on the wrong side of each long side of the trim. Press the trim to the shorts, centering the trim over the side seams. Apply the fusible tape to the wrong side of each piece of middy braid and press over the sides of the trim. Stitch if desired.

5 Fold the leg trim strips in half lengthwise and pin to the right side of the bottom of the shorts. Stitch. Open up the seam and topstitch with contrasting thread on the shorts ⅛" from the trim/shorts seam. Sew the inner leg seam with right side together.

6 Finish the top edge of the shorts by serging or with a zigzag stitch. Press this edge ⅝" to the wrong side and stitch ½" from the pressed edge, leaving an opening at the center back to insert elastic. Thread the elastic through the opening and secure the ends. Stitch the opening closed.

Day at the Beach

Lazy summer days are just right for lounging at the beach. Two-piece swimsuits are all the rage today. This doll-sized version is surprisingly easy to make. The fabric is a smooth Lycra print with binding made from a contrasting print. In this case, the plaid picks up two of the colors in the main print. Elastic is only necessary for the back leg openings of the swimsuit bottom.

The skirt and t-shirt ensemble is made using bright summer colors. The solid color t-shirt can be easily embroidered in many different designs to blend with the print of the skirt. The trendy "lettuce edge" treatment gives a soft, feminine look to the edges of the sleeves and hem of the shirt.

The beach towel tote bag is a handy way for your doll to carry her beach towel and other accessories. An embroidered felt pocket is applied to one end of a purchased hand towel. Straps for carrying are made from ribbon and attached to the towel and the felt pocket. When your doll is ready to go home, the towel can quickly be folded into the bag. Don't forget the sunscreen!

77

Two-Piece Swimsuit

Supplies:
⅛ yd. print Lycra fabric
⅛ yd. contrasting print fabric for binding
1" Velcro strip
4" elastic (⅛" wide)

Swimsuit Top

1 Cut one swimsuit top from the print Lycra fabric. Cut one strip ¾" x 3" for the top edge, one strip ¾" x 14½" for the lower edge, and two strips 1" x 17" for the straps from the contrasting Lycra fabric. These do not have to be cut on the bias since they have plenty of stretch.

2 With right sides together, sew the 3" strip to the top edge of the swimsuit. Fold the strip to the wrong side of the top edge and pin. Stitch over the previous seam on the right side, making sure to catch the strip underneath. Trim the strip close to the stitching on the wrong side.

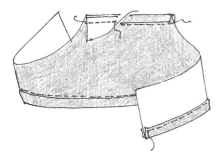

3 Sew the 14½" strip to the lower edge of the swimsuit, following the same instructions in Step 2.

American Girl doll

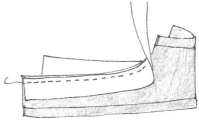

4 Sew the straps to the side edges of the top, beginning at the center back edges. Stitch in the same manner as the other strips until you come to the top of the swimsuit. Fold both of the long edges of the strip ¼" to the wrong side and stitch together, turning the short ends ¼" to the wrong side.

5 Fold the center back edges of the top ½" to the wrong side and stitch. Sew the Velcro to the back opening, lapping right over left.

6 Tie the straps behind the doll's neck.

Swimsuit Bottom

1 Cut one front and one back from the print Lycra fabric.

2 With right sides together, sew the crotch seam.

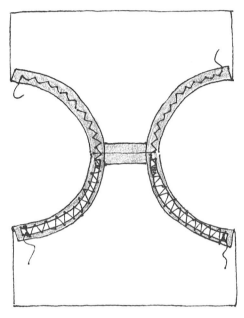

3 Fold the leg seam allowances ¼" to the wrong side and serge or zigzag stitch. Cut the elastic in half. Zigzag stitch one of the 2" pieces to a back leg opening only. Repeat with the other side.

4 Sew the side seams with right sides together.

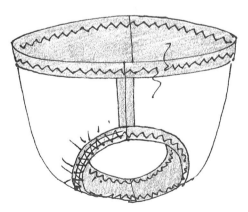

5 Fold the top edge of the swimsuit bottom to the wrong side and zigzag stitch.

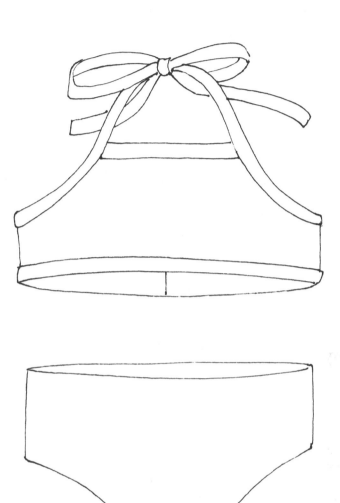

Summer Skirt and Lettuce-Edged T-Shirt

(designed by Lauri Cushing)

Supplies:
¼ yd. cotton knit fabric for the shirt
¼ cotton print fabric for the skirt
1½" x 8½" piece of knit ribbing
11" elastic (¼" wide)
4" Velcro strip
Optional: Swirled Sun embroidery design from *Doll Clothing Designs* by Joan Hinds from Cactus Punch, 2 colors 40 wt. embroidery thread, and stabilizer

Lettuce-Edged T-Shirt

1 Cut one front, two backs, and one neck ribbing from the knit fabric.

2 If you want to embroider the shirt, do so before construction. Place the front in the hoop over the stabilizer with the temporary spray adhesive. Embroider the design ½" to 1" below the neckline edge. Cut away the stabilizer.

3 With right sides together, sew the backs to the front at the shoulder seams.

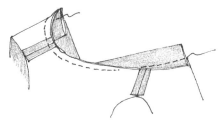

4 Fold the ribbing in half lengthwise with wrong sides together. Stretching the ribbing slightly, pin the ribbing to the

neckline and stitch. Press the center back seams, including the ribbing, ¼" to the wrong side and stitch.

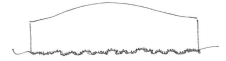

5 Using a wide zigzag stitch or a rolled hem stitch on a serger, stitch along the bottom edge of the sleeves, stretching slightly as you stitch. (If you are using a zigzag stitch, be sure that the needle goes off the fabric on the right hand side.) The edges will curl giving the sleeve edges a ruffled appearance.

6 Sew the sleeve caps to the armholes with right sides together, easing as necessary. Sew the underarm seams from the sleeve edges to the bottom of the shirt.

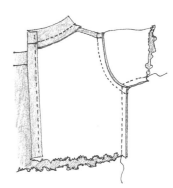

7 Using the same procedure as in Step 5, finish the hem of the shirt.

8 Sew the Velcro to the center back edges, lapping right over left.

Summer Skirt

1 Cut one front, one back, one waistband, and two pockets from the cotton print fabric.

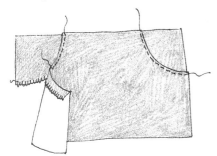

2 Serge or zigzag stitch the curved edges of the pockets to finish the edges. Press the curved pocket edge of the skirt ¼" to the wrong side. Place the pocket underneath the skirt pocket edge so that the top and side edges line up. Stitch close to the pressed pocket edge.

3 With right sides together, sew the side seams together.

4 Serge or zigzag stitch one long edge of the waistband. Sew the raw ends of the waistband with right sides together. Press seam allowances open.

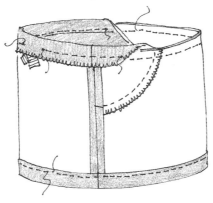

5 With right sides together, place the unstitched edge of the waistband on the skirt so that the seam of the waistband

aligns with the one of the side seams of the skirt. Stitch. Fold the waistband over to the inside of the skirt so the waistband is ½" wide. Topstitch in place, leaving a 1" opening at the back. Thread the elastic through the casing and secure the ends. Topstitch the opening closed.

6 Serge or zigzag stitch the hem of the skirt. Press it ¼" to the wrong side and stitch.

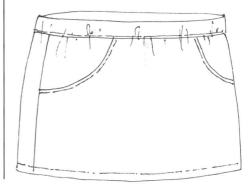

TIP

Sometimes it may be difficult to find the right fabric for a garment, especially if the type you are looking for is out of season. This was the case with the print fabric for the skirt. I found just what I wanted in the children's department of a discount store. You can purchase ready-made garments on sale for a reasonable price. If you choose to do this, be sure to buy the largest size possible. When the seams and other details are cut off, the usable fabric area may be smaller than you think.

Beach Towel Tote Bag

(designed by Marilee Sagat)

Supplies:

1 purchased hand towel
(approximately 16" x 24")

2 pieces contrasting color
felt large enough to fit in
embroidery hoop

44" grosgrain ribbon (¾" wide)

Fusible tape (¼" wide)

Optional: Fish embroidery design
from *Doll Clothing Designs* by
Joan Hinds from Cactus Punch
and 5 colors 40 wt. embroidery
thread

1 Increase the embroidery design by 20 percent. Embroider the design onto the center of each piece of felt. No stabilizer is necessary.

2 Cut each piece of felt 7" square, keeping the embroidery centered in the middle of the square. Cut the grosgrain ribbon in half.

3 Cut eight pieces of the fusible tape 6" long. Place two of the pieces along each side of the ribbon at the cut end. Iron the ribbon onto the felt, placing the ribbon 1½" from each side of the felt. Repeat

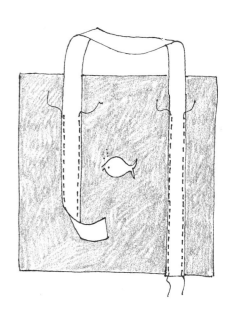

with the other end of the ribbon, placing it 1½" from the other side of the felt. The ribbon will loop at the top of the pocket. Stitch along both sides of the ribbon, making sure to only stitch 6" from the bottom of the pocket toward the top.

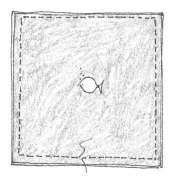

4 With wrong sides together, sew the pocket squares together ¼" and ⅛" along the edges of the pocket.

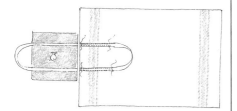

5 Iron on the fusible tape to the ends of the other piece of ribbon as done in Step 3. Place the felt pocket with the ribbon attached onto the center of the towel at one end. Using it as a placement guide, place the ribbon ends at the end of the towel so that the ribbon will loop as before. Iron the ribbon in place. Stitch

along both sides of the ribbon up only 6" from the end of the towel. Make sure that the needle thread matches the ribbon and the bobbin thread matches the towel.

6 Place the pocket unit with the ribbon handle on the towel directly over the ribbon handle on the towel. Topstitch ¼" and ⅛" along the sides and bottom edge.

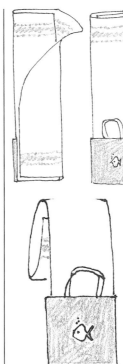

7 To fold the towel into the bag: with the back of the towel facing up, fold the towel in thirds from side to side. Pull the pocket from the backside of the towel and turn the pocket inside out. Fold the remaining end in thirds and continue folding into the pocket. The towel will have the appearance of emerging from the pocket.

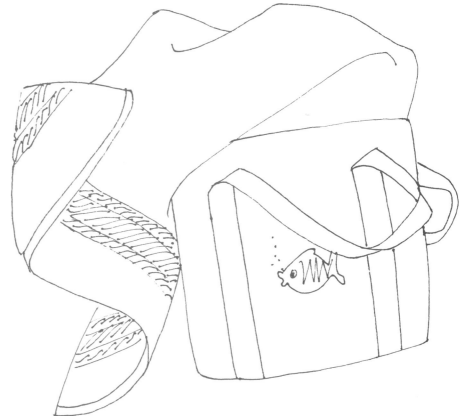

It's a Snow Day!

Göltz dolls

Playtime outdoors can be lots of fun in the winter. The dolls here have just the right clothing to be both warm and fashionable. One of the dolls wears a must-have fleece ensemble with lavender jeans. The heart print fleece jacket has a yoke and sleeves made from a solid coordinating color. The yoke front has heart motifs outlined on each side. The hearts are drawn on stabilizer and the outline is stitched with a reinforced straight stitch. This stitch goes back and forth over the stitching line twice. If you don't have this stitch built in your machine, simply stitch around the outline twice. This motif is echoed on the scarf and hat also. The jeans, made from lavender denim, pick up one of the colors in the jacket.

Another new fashion today is the jacket made from a suede-look fabric that has a fleecy type of backing. This jacket has unusual, but easy, construction techniques. The two seam allowances are placed over each other so that both suede sides of the fabric face up and overlap each other. This way the fleece side is seen at every seam line. Since no hems or seam finishes are needed, the collar does not have to be lined and the hemline is simply cut straight. The jacket closes with rectangular beads used as toggle buttons. The doll wears a trendy knitted hat called a "beanie." Mittens and a striped scarf will keep her warm and cozy. She wears these with the same double-knit pants seen with the lavender zippered-front sweater on page 21.

Skating is a great winter pastime. This doll is dressed in a competition skating costume. The costume is made from panne velvet, glittery Lycra, and sequin trim. The fitted costume opens in the back. Look for coordinating colors and patterns in both panne velvet and stretch velvet to pair with the Lycra fabric. The skirt can be optional.

Götz doll

Fleece Jacket, Hat, Scarf and Flared Jeans with Yoke

Fleece Jacket

Supplies:
¼ yd. solid fleece fabric
¼ yd. print fleece fabric
Contrasting 6" separating zipper
10" elastic (¼" wide)
Small piece of tear-away stabilizer
40 wt. rayon embroidery thread in a contrasting color

1 Cut two upper jacket fronts and two sleeves from the solid color fleece fabric. Cut two lower jacket fronts, one jacket back, and one collar from the print fleece fabric.

2 Trace the hearts on the upper front pattern piece onto the stabilizer. Place the stabilizer on each upper front as shown on the pattern piece and pin. Using the decorative embroidery thread, stitch around each heart with a reinforced straight stitch. (This stitch makes each stitch twice.) If you do not have this stitch on your machine, sew around each heart twice. Remove the stabilizer.

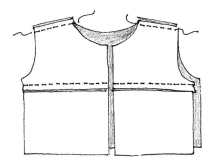

3 With right sides together, sew the lower fronts to the upper fronts. With right sides together, sew the fronts to the back at the shoulder seams.

4 Sew one long edge of the collar to the neck edge of the jacket with right sides together. Serge the other long edge of the collar, if desired.

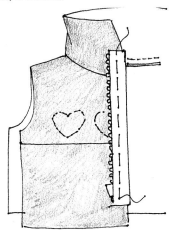

5 Place the wrong side of one-half of the zipper along the front opening.

The bottom of the zipper should be placed 1¼" from the lower edge of the jacket. (Zipper will only extend up approximately one half of the collar width. If the zipper fabric extends beyond one half of the width of the collar, trim off the excess.) Baste the zipper ¼" from the front edge. Open out the zipper to the right side and pin ¼" from the stitched seam, folding the collar to the inside over the zipper and covering the jacket/collar seam. Stitch, using a zipper or edge stitching presser foot. Repeat with the other side of the jacket and the other half of the zipper.

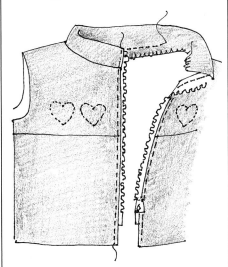

6 Pin the serged edge of the collar over the jacket/ collar seam line and stitch in the ditch to secure.

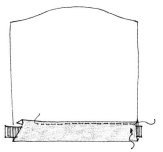

7 Fold the lower sleeve edges ¼" to the wrong side. Fold another ½" to form a casing. Stitch close to the fold. Cut 4" of elastic for each sleeve and thread through the casing. Secure at each side. With right sides together, pin the sleeves to the armholes, easing as necessary. Stitch.

8 Sew the underarm seams from the sleeve edge to the lower edge of the jacket.

9 Serge the lower edge of the jacket and pin this edge ¾" to the wrong side. Stitch ⅝" from the folded edge.

Hat and Scarf

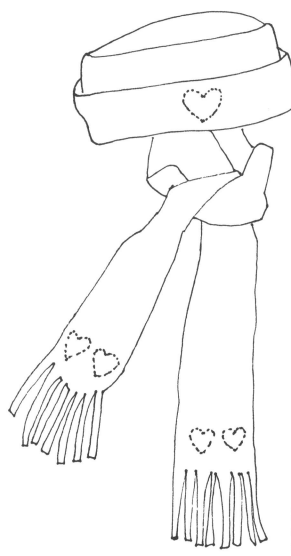

Supplies:
¼ yd. light-weight fleece fabric
40 wt. rayon embroidery thread in contrasting color
Small piece of tear-away stabilizer

Scarf

1 Cut the scarf 2½" x 25" from fleece fabric. With matching sewing thread, zigzag stitch or serge a rolled hem along the long sides of the scarf.

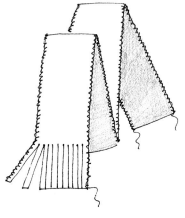

2 Measure 2½" from the short ends and mark this line with pins. Cut ¼" strips from the end of the scarf to the pin line to make fringe.

3 Trace the heart design onto the stabilizer. Pin the design 2¼" from the cut ends of the scarf. Using the embroidery thread, stitch the heart design as in Step 2 for the fleece jacket. Remove the stabilizer.

Hat

1 Cut one crown, one riser, and one brim from the fleece fabric.

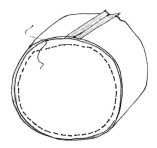

2 With right sides together, sew the short ends of the riser. Sew the crown to the top of the riser with right sides together.

3 Trace the heart design on the brim pattern piece onto the stabilizer. Place the stabilizer on the brim as shown on the pattern piece and pin. Using the decorative embroidery thread, stitch the heart design as in Step 2 on the previous page for the fleece jacket. Remove the stabilizer.

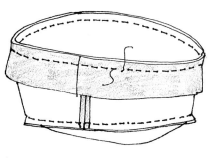

4 Sew the short ends of the brim with right sides together. Fold the brim in half lengthwise with wrong sides together. With the heart in the center front of the riser, stitch the right side of the brim to the wrong side of the riser. Fold the brim to the right side of the hat.

Flared Jeans with Yoke

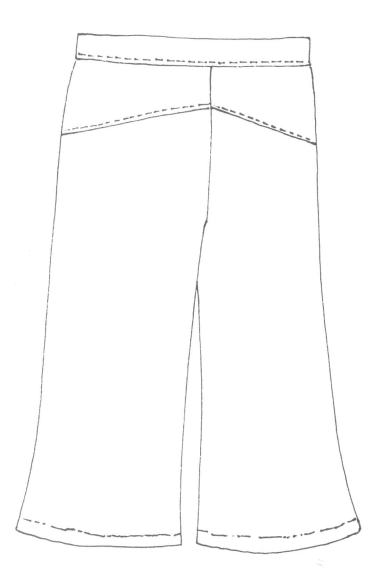

1 Cut two front yokes, two lower fronts, two backs, and one waistband from the fabric.

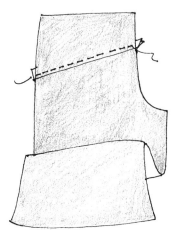

2 With right sides together, stitch the front yokes to the lower fronts. Press seam allowances to the top. With contrasting thread, topstitch a scant ⅛" above the seam.

3 Sew the center front and back seams and the side seams with right sides together.

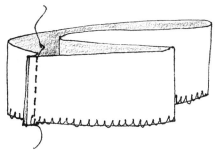

4 Serge or zigzag stitch along one long edge of the waistband. Stitch the short ends with right sides together. Press the seam allowances open.

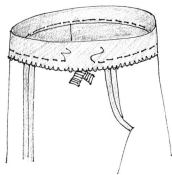

5 With right sides together, place the waistband on the jeans so that the seam of the waistband aligns with the center back seam of the jeans. Stitch. Fold the waistband over to the inside of the jeans so the waistband is ½" wide. Topstitch in place, leaving a 1" opening at the back. Thread the elastic through the casing and secure the ends. Topstitch the opening closed.

6 Serge or zigzag stitch along the lower edges of the jeans. Press the edges ½" to the wrong side. Stitch ⅜" from the pressed edge.

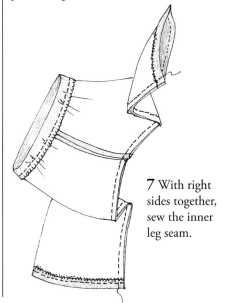

7 With right sides together, sew the inner leg seam.

Skater Costume

Supplies:
- ¼ yd. panne or stretch velvet fabric
- ¼ yd. Lycra fabric
- 9" elastic (¼" wide)
- ⅔ yd. sequin trim (⅜" wide)
- 3½" Velcro strip

1 Cut one upper front, two upper backs, and two sleeves from the Lycra fabric. Cut one lower front, one front panty, two lower backs, one back panty, and two skirts from the velvet fabric.

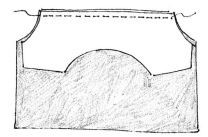

2 With right sides together, stitch the lower front to the upper front and the lower backs to the upper backs. Sew the front to the backs at the shoulder seams with right sides together.

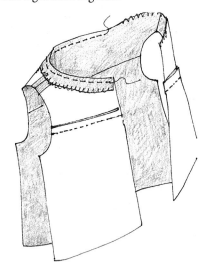

3 Turn the neck edge ¼" to the wrong side and stitch.

Götz doll

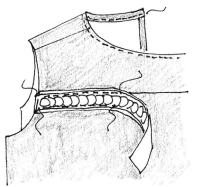

4 Stitch the sequin trim to the front over the seam line. Repeat with the backs. Turn the center back edges ¼" to the wrong side and stitch. Overlap the right back over the left back by ½" and stitch together along the seam line on the lower edge.

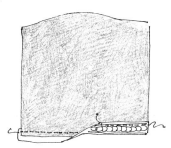

5 Place the wrong side of the trim over the right side of the lower edge of the sleeve. The trim will extend slightly beyond the lower sleeve edge. Stitch.

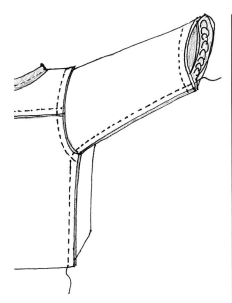

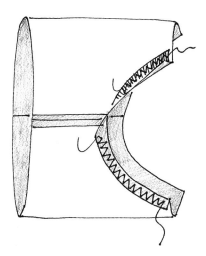

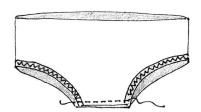

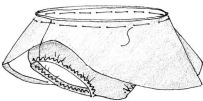

8 With right sides together, stitch the crotch seam.

6 Sew the sleeve caps to the armholes with right sides together. Sew the underarm seams from the sleeve edge to the bottom of the lower front and backs.

7 Stitch the front panty to the back panty at the side seams with right sides together. Cut the elastic in half and stretch each piece around the inside of the leg opening. The ends of the elastic should be flush with the fabric edges. Serge or zigzag stitch the elastic to the leg openings. Roll the elastic toward the inside of the leotard and zigzag stitch.

9 Turn the lower edges of the skirts ¼" to the wrong side and stitch. Sew the side seams with right sides together. Place the wrong side of the skirt over the right side of the panty and baste the top edges together. With right sides together, sew the panty/skirt combination to the top of the costume.

10 Sew the Velcro to the back opening.

TIP

The Skater Costume has elastic sewn to the leg openings to ensure a perfect fit. You can purchase clear elastic to use for this purpose. It may be a little wider, but it will not show from under the leg openings.

Suede Jacket, Knit Beanie, Long Striped Scarf and Garter Stitch Mittens

Götz doll

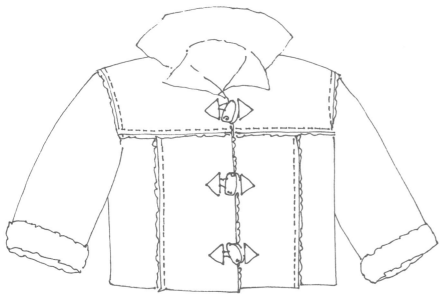

Suede Jacket

Supplies:
¼ yd. shearling suede fabric
3 rectangular wooden beads
    (6mm x 12mm)
12" leather lacing (⅛" wide)

Technique for sewing seams with shearling suede fabric:

The seams are not sewn in the traditional manner. The seam allowances overlap each other so the fleecy side of the fabric shows on the right side. To sew a seam, place a pin at the end of the seam to mark it. Place another pin at the end of the seam you are going to join. Place one of the pieces over the other matching the pin placement. Pin the seams together and stitch from the right side along the seam line.

1 Cut two upper fronts, two lower fronts, two lower side fronts, one upper back, one lower center back, two lower side backs, one collar, and two sleeves from the fabric.

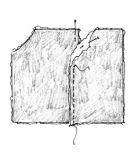

2 Using the above technique, sew the jacket lower fronts to the lower side fronts. Sew the lower center back to the lower side backs.

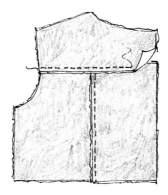

3 Sew the upper fronts to the lower fronts so that the upper front overlaps the lower front. Sew the upper back to the lower back in the same manner.

4 Sew the shoulder seams with the fronts overlapping the back.

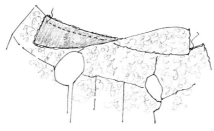

5 Place the collar on the center of the neckline with the right side of the collar on the wrong side, or fleece side of the jacket. (This step uses traditional sewing techniques.) Stitch.

6 Sew the sleeve caps to the armholes with the jacket overlapping the sleeves.

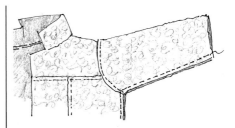

7 With right sides together, stitch the underarm seam from the sleeve edge to the bottom of the jacket, following traditional sewing techniques. Roll up the sleeve edges ¼".

8 Cut six triangular-shaped "patches" for the button loops and buttons. Cut as much of the fleece from the back of each patch as you can. Cut the lacing in half lengthwise so you have lacing that is about 1⁄16" wide. Cut six pieces 1¾" in length.

9 Thread the three beads onto the center of three of the laces. Fold the ends of the lacing together and wrap them with thread just below the beads to secure. Place the lacing ends under the patches and stitch to the jacket where marked on the pattern pieces.

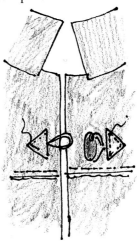

10 Fold the three other lacings in half to form a loop. Place the ends of the lacing under the patches and stitch to the other side of the jacket as marked on the pattern pieces. Be sure that the bead can slip through the loop.

11 Trim the bottom of the jacket, if necessary, so that all edges are even.

Knit Beanie

(designed by Lauri Cushing)

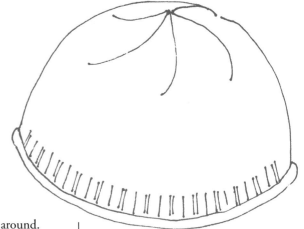

Supplies:

50 gm ball of sport weight yarn*
1 set of double-pointed needles, size 3
Tapestry needle

*Used in this project: Wildflower cotton

Gauge: 7 sts per inch.

Cast on 80 sts. Join and knit 4 rounds
K2, P2, ribbing for 4 rounds.
K 12 rounds (about 1¼" above the ribbing).
*K7, K 2 tog, repeat from * for a total of 8 times.
K one round.
*K6, K 2 tog, repeat from * around.
K one round.

*K5, K 2 tog, repeat from * around.
K one round.
*K4, K 2 tog, repeat from * around.
K one round.
*K3, K 2 tog, repeat from * around.
K one round.
*K2, K 2 tog, repeat from * around.
K one round.
*K1, K 2 tog, repeat from * around.
K one round.
K 2 tog all the way around.

Cut yarn leaving an 8" tail. Thread the yarn through a tapestry needle and draw up remaining sts. Hide the ends.

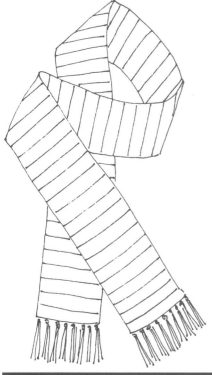

Long Striped Scarf

(designed by Lauri Cushing)

Supplies:

Fingering weight sock yarn in 2 colors *
Size 2 straight needles

*Used in this project: Wildfoote

Gauge: not important

Cast on 16 sts. Work in K1, P1 ribbing for the entire scarf.
Knit 2 rows with one color and then change to the next color.
Continue to change colors after two rows. Knit the first st of the color change row with both the old and new color. On the next row, knit with both together as one st. This will carry your yarn up the side of the scarf in a tidy way.
Knit for 22".
Cut 16 pieces of yarn 5" long for the fringe. Tie to each end of the scarf. Trim the fringe to even the ends.

TIP

The scarf will also work up well in a patterned multicolored sock yarn. If you work in the ribbing as instructed for the striped scarf, you won't need to change colors. The yarn will do it for you!

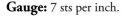

Garter Stitch Mittens

(designed by Lauri Cushing)

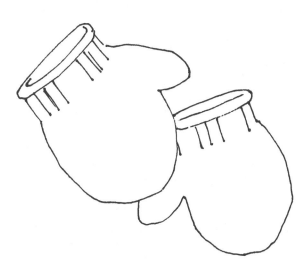

Supplies:

½ oz. sport weight yarn*

4 sets of double-pointed needles, size 2

*Used in this project: Wildflower cotton

Gauge: 5 sts per inch in garter st (knit 1 round, purl 1 round).

Cast on 20 sts. Join and knit 4 rounds.
Knit 2, purl 2 ribbing for 4 rounds.
Knit 1 row, purl 1 row.

Thumb gusset:

Round 1: M1, K1, M1. Place a marker. Knit to the end of the round.

Round 2: Purl one round.

Repeat these 2 rounds, knitting the extra between the M1's until 7 sts are before the marker. Place these sts on a toothpick. Cast on 1 st at the end of the round. Continue in garter st for 10 rounds.

Shape the tip: Knit 1, knit 2 tog all the way around.

Purl 2 together around.

Leave a 4" tail and cut yarn. Thread through remaining stitches and draw closed.

Thumb:

Put 7 thumb sts on 2 needles and pick up 3 sts over cast on sts. On the next round, decrease those to 1 st. Work 4 rounds in garter st. Knit 1, knit 2 together around. Purl 2 together around. Draw up as on the body of the mitten.

Make another mitten.

Pajama Party

From left to right: Creative Doll Company, Götz, and Laura Ashley dolls

Dolls just want to have fun, especially at sleepovers. These dolls have a great bedtime wardrobe, but you can be sure not much sleeping will be done! The doll sitting on the floor wears shiny satin pajamas with an Asian-style side closure, even though the top opens in the back. The striped satin fabric in the pants coordinates with the colors in the animal print top and is trimmed with bright pink rickrack.

Another doll wears a cozy flannel nightgown that has a very contemporary look. The scoop neck has a ruffle and a self-bias binding. The sleeves are full, but the sleeve caps are not gathered. This follows today's fashion trends. Another ruffle edges the bottom of the nightgown.

The last doll wears matching satin PJs and a floor-length robe with a moon-and-stars print. The PJ tank top is trimmed with the print fabric along the neckline and straps. The front of the top has a machine embroidered moon and star motif that complements the fabric print. The print robe has pockets with the same embroidery that has been reduced in size.

Laura Ashley doll

Satin Pajamas

Supplies:

¼ yd. animal print flannel-backed satin fabric

¼ yd. striped flannel-backed satin fabric

1 yd. rickrack

3" Velcro strip

11" elastic (¼" wide)

Pajama Top

1 Cut one lower front, one upper front, two backs, two collars, and two sleeves from the animal print fabric.

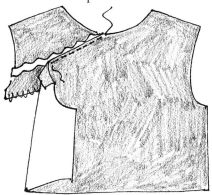

2 Serge or zigzag stitch the center front and lower edge of the upper front. Press the angled edge of the lower front ¼" to the wrong side. Place the wrong side of the pressed lower front edge over the right side of the upper front on the line marked on the pattern piece. Cut a piece of rickrack to fit under the folded edge so that just the peaks of the rickrack extend. Stitch.

3 With right sides together, stitch the shoulder seams. Press seam allowances open. Serge or zigzag stitch the center back edges. Press them ¼" to the wrong side and stitch.

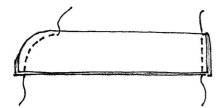

4 Fold each collar in half lengthwise on the fold line with right sides together. Stitch both the curved and straight ends of each collar.

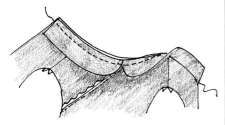

Clip the curves, turn to the right side, and press. With right sides together, pin the collars to the neckline edge so that the curved ends meet at the center front. Stitch. Topstitch on the top close to the seam so that the collar will stand up.

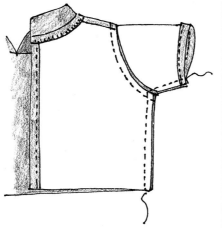

5 Serge or zigzag stitch the lower edges of the sleeves. Press them ¼" to the wrong side and stitch. With right sides together, sew the sleeve caps to the armholes, easing as necessary. Sew the underarm seam from the sleeve edge to the lower edge of the pajama top.

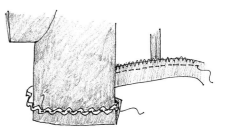

6 Serge or zigzag stitch the hem edge of the pajama top. Press this edge ½" to the wrong side and stitch ⅜" from the fold. Sew rickrack over the stitching, turning the ends under at the center back edges.

7 Sew the Velcro to the back opening, lapping right over left.

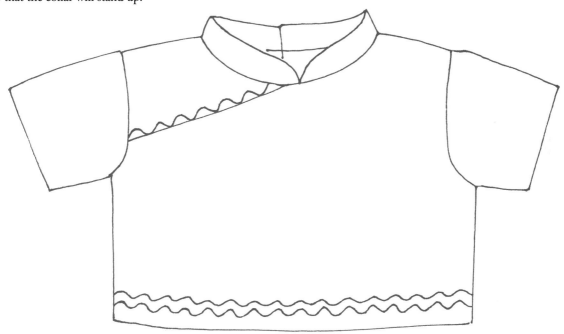

Pajama Pants

1 Cut four pants from the striped fabric. Cut two cuffs from the animal print fabric.

2 With right sides together, stitch two pants together at the side seam. Repeat with the remaining two pants.

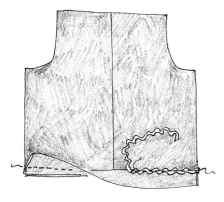

3 Fold the cuffs in half lengthwise with wrong sides together and press. Stitch each cuff to the pants at the lower edge with right sides together and press. Stitch a piece of rickrack over the seam line on both pants.

4 With right sides together, sew the center front and center back seams. Sew the inner leg seam.

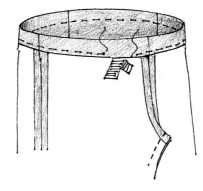

5 Press the top edge of the pants ¼" to the wrong side. Press again another ½" and stitch to make a casing, leaving a 1" opening at the center back. Thread the elastic through the opening and secure the ends. Stitch the opening closed.

TIP

Sewing with satin can sometimes be difficult since it has a tendency to slip. Satin fabric designed for sleepwear is often backed with flannel, which will make slippage less of a problem. If you are using a slippery satin fabric, be sure to use sharp pins and needles to prevent any snagging. To prevent slippage while sewing, pin carefully and often. You may even try to put the pins in opposite directions on the seam line. Remember to set your iron on a low setting.

Götz doll

Flannel
Nightgown

Supplies:
½ yd. printed flannel fabric
3" Velcro strip
8" elastic (⅛" wide)

1 Cut one front, two backs, two sleeves, one neckline ruffle, one hemline ruffle, and one bias strip 1" x 11½" from the fabric.

2 Serge or zigzag stitch the center back edges separately. With right sides together, sew the center back seam to the dot marked on the pattern piece. Press the seam allowances open, including the unstitched part of the seam, and topstitch the open area of the seam.

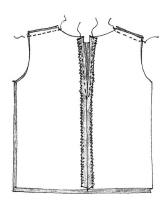

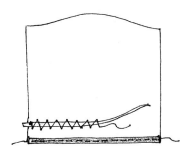

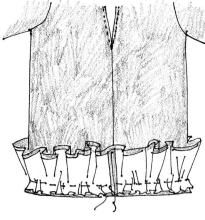

3 Sew the front to the backs at the shoulder seams with right sides together. Press seam allowances open.

4 Narrow hem one long edge of the neckline ruffle. Press the short ends of the ruffle ¼" to the wrong side and stitch. Gather the unfinished edge of the ruffle to fit the neckline. Place the wrong side of the ruffle to the right side of the neck edge and baste.

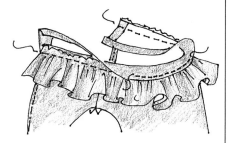

5 Press one of the long edges of the bias strip ¼" to the wrong side. Pin the right side of the unpressed long edge of the bias to the wrong side of neckline so that the short ends of the strip extend ¼" beyond the nightgown. Stitch. Fold the binding over to the outside of the garment, enclosing the short ends. Pin carefully and topstitch.

6 Press the lower edge of the sleeves ¼" to the wrong side and stitch. Cut the elastic in half. Measure ½" from the hemmed edge along one side of the sleeve and stitch the elastic with two to three straight stitches to secure. With a wide zigzag stitch, sew the elastic to the sleeve ½" above the lower edge. Stretch the elastic as you stitch. When you reach the other side, secure with two to three straight stitches.

7 With right sides together, stitch the sleeve caps to the armholes, easing as necessary. Sew the underarm seam from the sleeve edge to the bottom of the nightgown.

8 Narrow hem one long edge of the hemline ruffle. With right sides together, sew the short ends together. Gather the unfinished edge of the ruffle to fit the bottom of the nightgown. Stitch to the nightgown with right sides together.

9 Sew the Velcro to the back opening, lapping right over left.

TIP

When working with tiny curved seams, an easy way to clip the curves is to trim the seam slightly with a pinking sheers. This will eliminate the danger of clipping into the seam line. You can even cut out the pattern pieces with a pinking sheers if you like.

PJs and Robe

(designed by Marilee Sagat)

Supplies:

½ yd. yellow flannel-backed satin

½ yd. print flannel-backed satin

2" Velcro strip

11" elastic (¼" wide)

Optional: Moon and Stars embroidery design from *Doll Clothing Designs* by Joan Hinds for Cactus Punch, 2 colors of 40 wt. embroidery thread, and tear-away stabilizer

PJs

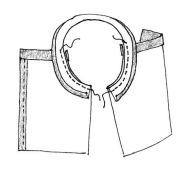

1 Trace the top front onto a piece of the solid color fabric large enough to fit in your embroidery hoop. Enlarge the embroidery design by 20 percent so that it measures 41mm high x 43mm wide. Center the design 1½" from the top front edge and embroider according to your sewing machine's instructions. Tear off the stabilizer and cut out the front.

2 Cut two top backs and four pajama bottoms from the solid fabric. Cut two bias strips of the print fabric 1" x 8" for the straps. Cut one bias strip 1½" x 8" for the front and back top edges.

3 Fold the center back edges ¼" to the wrong side and stitch. Cut a 1½" piece of bias from one of the strips to fit the top front edge. Press one long edge ¼" to the wrong side. Stitch the right side of the unpressed edge of the strip to the wrong side of the top. Fold the strip over to the right side and stitch close to the pressed edge.

4 Cut the rest of the strip in half. Press one long edge and one short end ¼" to the wrong side. Stitch the right side of the unpressed edge of the strip to the wrong side of the back edge, placing the pressed short end flush with the center back seam. Fold the strip over to the right side and stitch close to the pressed edge. Repeat with the remaining strip half and the other back edge.

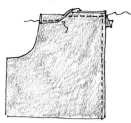

5 Pin the right side of one of the remaining bias strips to the wrong side of one of the front armholes, beginning at the side seam.

When you reach the top, measure 3" of the strip and mark. Resume pinning the strip to the back armhole at this mark and pin around the rest of the armhole. Stitch.

6 Fold the strip over to the right side of the front and back armholes, tucking in the raw edge ¼" to the wrong side. On the 3" strap area, press both of the raw edges ¼" to the wrong side and press again so that the pressed edges meet. Pin securely and stitch. Repeat with the other armhole.

7 Sew the side seams with right sides together.

8 Serge or zigzag stitch the lower edge of the top. Press this edge ½" to the wrong side and stitch ⅜" from the edge.

9 Lapping right over left, sew Velcro to the center back opening.

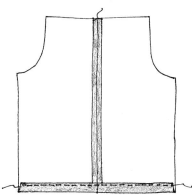

10 For the pajama bottoms, stitch the center front and back seams with right sides together.

11 Stitch the front to the back at the side seams with right sides together.

12 Hem pajama bottoms by pressing the edge ¼" to the wrong side. Press again another ¼" and stitch.

13 Press the top edge of the pajama bottoms ¼" to the wrong side. Press again another ½" and stitch close to the fold, leaving 1" opening near the back seam. Insert elastic into casing and secure ends by overlapping slightly. Stitch the opening closed.

14 With right sides together, sew the inner leg seam.

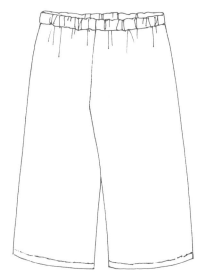

edge of the robe and baste, centering the collar over the center back of the robe.

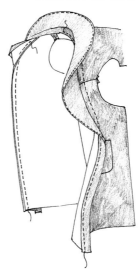

7 Press one long edge of the bias strip ¼" to the wrong side. With right sides together, stitch the unpressed edge to one center front, around the neckline, and down the other center front. Clip the curves and press the bias to the inside of the robe. Topstitch close to the edge of the bias.

8 Serge or zigzag stitch the bottom of each sleeve. Press this edge ¾" to the wrong side and stitch. With right sides together, sew the sleeves to the robe armholes.

9 Sew the underarm seam from the wrist to the dot marked on the side seams of the pattern piece. Press the seam allowances open, including the unstitched part.

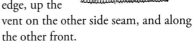

10 Serge or zigzag stitch the bottom edge of the robe, press ¼" to the wrong side, and stitch along the front edge, up the vents on the side seam, along the back edge, up the vent on the other side seam, and along the other front.

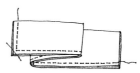

Robe

1 Trace a pocket onto a piece of the solid color fabric large enough to fit into your embroidery hoop. Reduce the embroidery design by 20 percent so that it measures approximately 27mm high x 28mm wide. Center the design on the pocket and embroider according to your sewing machine's instructions. Tear off the stabilizer and cut out the pocket. Embroider a second pocket and cut out.

2 Cut one back, two fronts, and two sleeves from the print fabric. Cut two collars, one belt, two pocket linings, and a 1" x 36" bias strip from the yellow fabric.

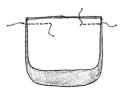

3 To make each pocket, sew the pocket and lining with right sides together along the top edge only, leaving a 1" opening in the center of the seam.

Press the entire seam allowance toward the pocket lining. Match the pocket and lining side and bottom edges and stitch with right sides together. Clip the curves and turn to the right side. Turn the pocket to the right side through the hole left in the top of the pocket and press. Slipstitch the opening closed.

4 Pin the pockets to each robe front as shown on the pattern piece. Stitch close to the side and bottom edges.

5 Sew the back to the fronts at the shoulder seams with right sides together.

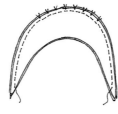

6 With right sides together, sew the collar to its lining around the outside edge. Clip the curves, turn to the right side, and press. Topstitch ¼" from the pressed edge. Pin the collar to the neck

11 Fold the belt in half lengthwise with right sides together. Stitch along one long edge and one short end. Trim the corner and turn to the right side. Slipstitch the remaining end closed. Tie around the waist.

All Dressed Up

From left to right: American Girl and Götz dolls

The cool winter months are loaded with holiday parties. These dolls are ready for any special event that comes along! The first doll has just arrived at the party wearing a double-breasted coat and hat. The wool coat has a fake fur collar and cuffs. The unique felted hat is knitted first with wool yarn. It is then "felted" by washing in hot water. It is dried on a form, such as a plastic bottle that is approximately the shape of the doll's head. The flower that decorates the brim is made from a length of gathered satin.

The winter party dress, worn by the next doll, features a stretch velvet bodice. This fabric is very popular with girls today for holiday dresses. The dress has a scoop neck and long, straight sleeves. The skirt has an overskirt of a sparkly sheer organza trimmed with ribbon that matches the bodice. Her necklace is simply a ribbon threaded through a doll-sized belt buckle with a jewel glued in the center. This is a great project to enlist the help of young doll lovers in your household!

Another high-fashion holiday outfit is the Asian-Style Dress. The wonderful cotton fabric has a small print with fans and is accented with gold. The mandarin collar and side opening are finished with gold piping and tiny doll-sized cord frog closures. This dress can be shortened and worn over jeans or dress pants for another classic look.

Götz doll

Dress Coat and Felted Hat

Dress Coat

Supplies:
½ yd. lightweight wool fabric
½ yd. matching fabric for lining
¼ yd. faux fur for collar and cuffs
6 buttons (⅜")
3 small snaps

1 Cut two fronts, one back, and two sleeves from the wool fabric. Cut two fronts and one back from the lining fabric. Cut one collar and two cuffs from both the fur and lining fabrics.

2 With right sides together, sew the shoulder seams of the wool fabric. Repeat with the lining fabric. Press the seam allowances open.

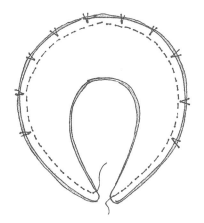

3 Sew the collar to the collar lining around the curved outside edge with right sides together. Clip the curves and turn to the right side. Press from the lining side only. Pin the collar to the right side of the neck edge of the coat and baste.

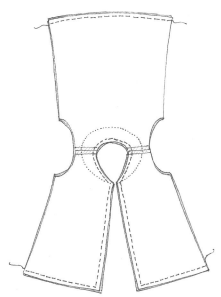

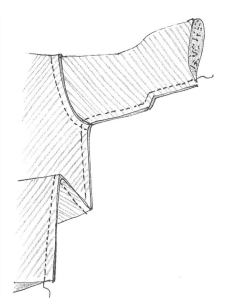

6 Sew the underarm seams from the sleeve edge to hem of the coat.

7 Sew the buttons to the right front of the coat as shown on the pattern piece. Sew one half of each snap on the left front as marked on the pattern piece. The other snap halves are stitched underneath the three buttons closest to edge of the coat.

Pin the lining to the coat with right sides together and stitch along the center front edges, around the neckline, and along the hem edges of the fronts and back. (The ends of the collar will be caught in the seams.) Clip the curves, turn to the right side, and press. Stitch the lining to the coat just under the collar so it will lay flat.

4 Pin the lining to the coat around the armholes and baste.

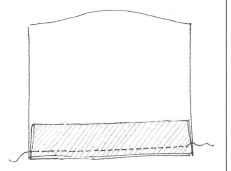

5 Sew the lining to the sleeve cuffs along one long edge with right sides together. Turn right-side out and press on the lining side. Stitch the right side of the cuff to the wrong side of the sleeve edge. Fold the cuff to the right side of the sleeve and baste along the side edges. With right sides together, sew the sleeves to the armholes.

Felted Hat

(designed by Ceci Riehl)

Supplies:

Yarn Requirements: About 30 gm worsted weight, non-washable wool. Only non-machine-washable wools will felt. (Look for wools that specify cold-water washing.) The dark colors felt better than very light colors.

Needles: A 16" or 11" circular needle #8. Set of #8 double pointed needles. A set of double-pointed needles may be used for the whole project if you prefer.

Abbreviations and terms used:
K2tog—Knit two sts together as one.
M1—(Make one) Insert left needle from front to back, under the horizontal strand between the st on left needle and the st just worked, forming a loop on left needle. Knit this loop through the back.
Stockinette st—Knit every round.

Using the circular needle, cast on 90 sts. Join into a round, being careful not to twist the sts around the needle. Do this by transferring the last st onto the other end of the needle. Then pull the first st over this st and put it on the left hand needle. Work this st as the first.

Knit one round. Place a marker at the beginning of the round.
Next round: *K9, M1* repeat around (100 sts).
Knit in rounds of stockinette st until work measures **1½**" from cast on edge.
Next round: *K8, K2tog* repeat around (90 sts).
Knit in stockinette st another 1½" (**3**" from cast on edge).

Beginning of crown:
Round 1: *(K2tog) 4 times, K1* repeat around (50 sts).
Round 2: Knit around.

Round 3: *K2, M1, K3, M1* repeat around (70 sts).
Continue knitting in stockinette st until work measures 3½" from beginning of crown.
Begin top decreases:
Change to double pointed needles when necessary.
Round 1: *K5, K2tog* repeat around (60 stitches).
Round 2 and all even rounds: Knit around.
Round 3: *K4, K2tog* repeat around (50 stitches).
Round 5: *K3, K2tog* repeat around (40 stitches).
Round 7: *K2, K2tog* repeat around (30 stitches).
Round 9: *K1, K2tog* repeat around (20 stitches).
Round 11: *K2tog* repeat around (10 stitches).
Cut yarn, leaving an 18" tail. With tapestry needle, thread yarn through the remaining sts and pull together. Fasten off. Work in all yarn ends.

Felting instructions:

1 Place hat in a zippered pillow case protector or a pillowcase tied shut with a strong rubber band may work.

2 Set washer to hot wash, small load size, and longest cycle. Add a small amount of laundry detergent. Put the pillowcase in the washer with another heavy lint-free item, such as an old pair of jeans. Let the cycle run to the end.

3 Take the hat out and check its size. Try it on your doll. If it is still too big, repeat the above process. Two or three cycles should be enough, but if it isn't shrinking enough, keep trying.

4 When it seems to be the right size, let it dry. It is helpful to put it over an object about the size of your doll's head, such as a plastic lemonade mix container.

Flower

Supplies:
1½" x 36" satin fabric to match the
    color of the coat
Fast drying glue, such as Fabri-tac

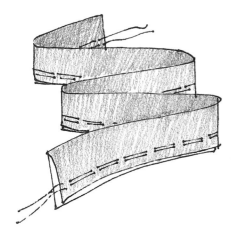

1 Fold the fabric strip in half lengthwise
with wrong sides together. Sew two rows
of gathering threads along the cut edges.

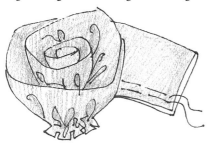

2 Pull the gathering threads tightly at
one end to make a tight circle. With a
hand-sewing needle and thread, tack the
bottom of the flower with a few stitches
to hold it together. Keep wrapping the
fabric around the center until you have
approximately 1" of fabric left. Tuck the
fabric under and stitch to the bottom of
the flower.

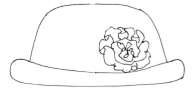

3 Use glue to attach the flower to the
brim of the hat.

Götz doll

Götz doll

Winter Party Dress

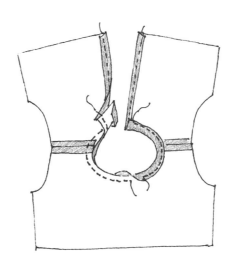

Supplies:

¼ yd. stretch velvet fabric

¼ yd. iridescent organza fabric

¼ yd. taffeta or crinoline fabric

10½" single-fold bias tape

1¼ yd. ribbon (⅜" wide)

1 yd. ribbon for sash (⅞" wide)

5 purchased ribbon roses
   (1" wide) to match sash ribbon

3" Velcro strip

1 Cut one front, two backs, and two sleeves from the stretch velvet fabric. Cut the skirt 7½" x 45" from both the taffeta and the organza.

2 With right sides together, sew the front to the backs at the shoulder seams. Press seam allowances open. Press the center back edges ¼" to the wrong side and stitch.

3 With right sides together, pin the bias tape to neckline edge with the short ends extending ¼" beyond the center back edges. Stitch. Fold the bias to the inside of the garment, tucking in the short ends, and stitch.

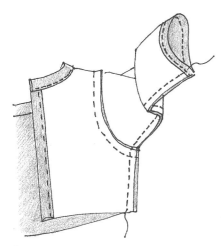

4 Press the sleeve edges ¼" to the wrong side and stitch. Sew the sleeve caps to the armholes with right sides together. Sew the underarm seam from the sleeve edge to the bottom of the bodice.

5 Narrow hem one long edge of the taffeta skirt. With right sides together, sew the short ends of the skirt together to within 3" from the top. Press the seam

allowances open, including the unstitched part, and top stitch around the opening.

6 Press one long edge of the organza skirt ¼" to the right side. Place the ⅜" ribbon over the pressed edge and stitch along both sides of the ribbon. Sew the short ends together as in Step 5.

7 Place the wrong side of the organza skirt to the right side of the satin skirt, lining up the hemmed edges and the center back seam. From now on, the skirts will be treated as one. Gather the top edge to fit the bodice. Sew the skirt to the bodice with right sides together.

8 Lapping right over left, sew the Velcro to the back opening.

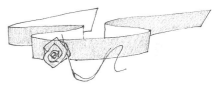

9 Sew the ribbon roses to the center of the sash ribbon, and tie it around the waist.

TIP

Gathered skirts look best when they stand out as full as they can. The Winter Party Dress uses a very stiff crinoline fabric for the underskirt that does not easily flatten. It is white and will look like taffeta under organza or other sheer fabric. If you want to have a different color skirt, you can make an underskirt from the crinoline and an overskirt of another color satin, cotton, or other fabric.

Asian-Style Dress

1 Cut one lower front, one upper front, two backs, two sleeves, and four collars from the print fabric.

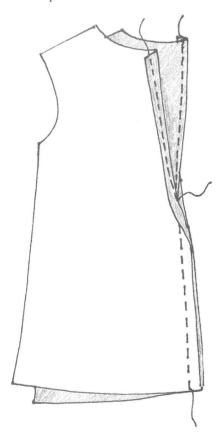

2 With right sides together, stitch the center back seam to the dot indicated on the pattern piece. Press the seam allowances open, including the unstitched part. Topstitch around the opening.

American Girl Girl doll

3 Fold the lamé strip over the cording and sew close to the cord using a piping foot or zipper foot on the sewing machine. Trim the seam allowance to ¼".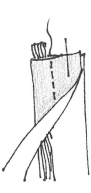

4 Serge or zigzag stitch the center front and lower edge of the upper front. Cut a piece of piping to fit the angled edge of the lower front. Stitch to the lower front with right sides together.

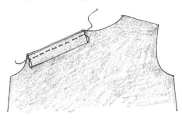

Press the seam allowance of the angled edge of the lower front to the wrong side. Place the wrong side of the pressed lower front edge over the right side of the upper front on the center front line marked on the pattern piece.

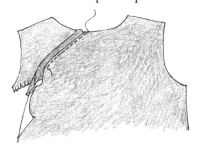

Stitch in the ditch of the piping/lower front seam to attach it to the upper front.

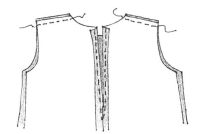

5 With right sides together, stitch the shoulder seams. Press seam allowances open.

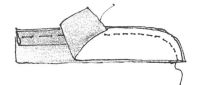

6 Cut a piece of piping to fit the curved edge of one of the collars. With right sides together, baste the piping to the collar. Sew another collar to the piped collar along the curved and center back edges with right sides together. Turn to the right side and press. Repeat with the other collar pieces.

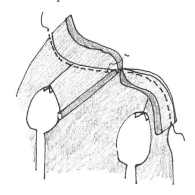

7 Place the collars on the neckline of the dress so that they meet at the center front. Stitch. Serge or zigzag stitch the

seam allowances. Press the collar seam allowances toward the dress. Topstitch on the dress close to the seam so that the collar will stand up.

8 Serge or zigzag stitch the lower edges of the sleeves. Press them ¼" to the wrong side and stitch. With right sides together, sew the sleeve caps to the armholes, easing as necessary. Sew the underarm seam from the sleeve edge to the hem edge of the dress.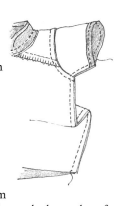

9 Serge or zigzag stitch the lower edge of the dress and press it ¼" to the wrong side. Stitch ⅛" from the pressed edge.

10 Hand-stitch the two mini-cord closures over the piped front seam as shown in the photo.

11 Lapping right over left, sew the Velcro to the back opening.

Special Occasions

Springtime brings many special events for girls. Dolls can have their own miniaturized versions of these special occasion clothes as well. One lucky doll wears a flower girl dress and floral wreath. The fabric for the dress is pale pink satin with matching sheer organza. The bodice has a high sheer organza yoke and sleeves. The full skirt features a sheer organza overskirt. The belt is pleated satin with ribbon ties. Gathered satin and a covered button provide just the right trim for the ensemble.

First Communion is celebrated with a white dress and short veil. The outfit shown here is very similar to the flower girl dress. The yoke is made from the satin, however, so it doesn't appear sheer. The overskirt is made from lace fabric that has a scalloped edge on the selvedge. You will cut along this edge for the skirt instead of widthwise, so be sure you purchase enough fabric. The netting and ribbon veil is attached to a barrette for easy placement at the back of the doll's head.

The aqua fabrics and daisy trim make the perfect combination for celebrating spring holidays. Daisy trim, first popular in the 60s, is often seen in clothing today. The short-sleeved bodice is sewn from a dotted fabric that matches the daisy and checked fabric for the skirt. The belt is made by covering ribbon with daisy trim that is sold by the yard. Her necklace is a small, jeweled heart found in the girl's jewelry section of stores. It is placed on a silver chain found in craft stores. Shorten the chain to 8" and apply clasps to each end.

Flower Girl

Supplies:

⅓ yd. satin fabric

⅓ yd. sheer organza fabric

3" x 8" piece of light-weight lining fabric for the sash

30" satin ribbon (⅞" wide)

3" Velcro strip

1 button to cover (⁷⁄₁₆" or ½")

1 Cut a 4" x 20" piece of satin and organza fabric and a 3" x 20" piece of organza fabric. Place the wrong side of the wider organza over the right side of the wider satin and baste the long edges together. With right sides together, stitch both of the strips together along one long edge. Press the seam allowance toward the satin.

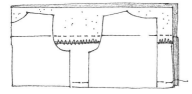

2 Place the back bodice pattern piece over the pieced fabric so that the fabric seam is under the line drawn on the pattern piece. Cut another back bodice piece using the same method, but be sure to flip the pattern piece over. Fold the remaining fabric in half widthwise and cut the front bodice the same way. Cut two sleeves, one bias neckline binding 1" x 8½", and a skirt 9" x 45" from the organza.

Cut another skirt from the satin. Cut one sash from the satin and one from the lining fabric. Cut one flower from the satin.

Götz doll

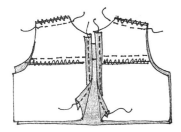

3 With right sides together, sew the shoulder seams of the bodice. Finish seam allowances and press to the back. Serge or zigzag stitch the center back opening and press ¼" to the wrong side. Stitch.

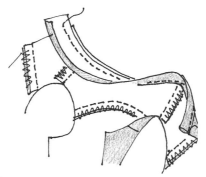

4 Press one long edge of the bias binding ¼" to the wrong side. Pin the right side of the unpressed edge of the binding to the wrong side of the neckline with the short ends extending by ¼". Stitch. Fold the binding to the right side and stitch, tucking in the short ends.

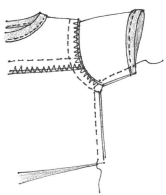

5 Narrow hem the lower edges of the sleeves. With right sides together, sew the sleeve caps to the armholes, easing as necessary. Stitch the underarm seams from the sleeve edges to the bottom of the bodice.

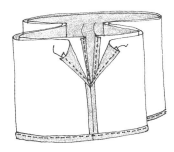

6 Narrow hem one long edge of the organza skirt. With right sides together, sew the short ends together to within 3" from the top. Press the seam allowances open, including the unstitched part, and top stitch around the opening. Repeat with the satin skirt. Place the wrong side of the organza skirt to the right side of the satin skirt, lining up the hemmed edges and the center back seam. From now on, the skirts will be treated as one.

7 Gather the top of the skirt to fit the bodice. With right sides together, stitch the skirt to the lower edge of the bodice.

8 Sew the Velcro to the back opening, lapping right over left.

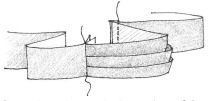

9 For the sash, sew the long edges of the satin and lining with right sides together. Turn to the right side and press. Press two equally spaced ½" pleats lengthwise in the sash. (The width of the sash will be the same as the ribbon width.) Baste the short ends to hold the pleats. Cut the ribbon in half. Stitch one end to the short, raw end of the sash, with right sides together.

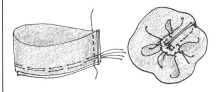

10 Fold the flower piece in half lengthwise, but do not press. Gather the cut edges and pull tightly. Sew the raw ends with right sides together, which will make a circle.

Cover the button with satin, following the manufacturer's instructions. Stitch to the center of the flower. Sew the flower to the sash 1" from the center. Tie the sash around the waist.

Flower Wreath

Supplies:
32" of 30-gauge green fabric-covered wire
14 small flower bunches

1 Wrap the wire around each flower bunch at 1" intervals.

2 Wire the ends together when the circle measures 15" long.

Spring Party Dress

American Girl doll

Supplies:
¼ yd. pastel dot print fabric
¼ yd. pastel check fabric to match
⅓ yd. daisy lace trim (1⅛" wide)
1 yd. ribbon (⅞" wide)
3" Velcro strip

1 Cut two fronts, four backs, and two sleeves from the dotted fabric. Cut one skirt 8¼" x 45" from the checked fabric.

2 With right sides together, sew a front to two backs at the shoulder seams. Press seam allowances open. Repeat with the other set for the lining.

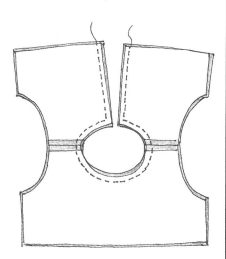

3 With right sides together, sew the bodice to its lining around the neckline and down the center backs. Clip the curves, trim the seam, and turn to the right side. Press.

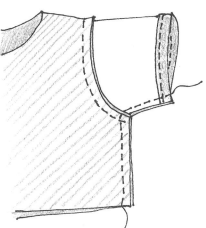

4 Serge or zigzag stitch the lower edges of the sleeves. Press the sleeve edges ¼" to the wrong side and stitch. Sew the sleeve caps to the armholes with right sides together, easing as necessary. Sew the underarm seam from the sleeve edge to the bottom of the bodice.

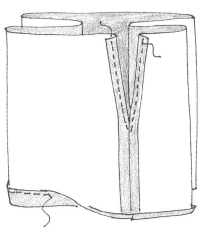

5 Press one long edge of the skirt ¼" to the wrong side. Press again another ¾" and stitch. With right sides together, sew the short ends of the skirt together to within 3" from the top. Press the seam allowances open, including the unstitched part, and top stitch around the opening.

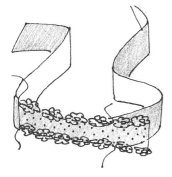

6 Gather the top of the skirt to fit the bodice. With right sides together, sew the bodice to the skirt.

7 Lapping right over left, sew the Velcro to the back opening.

8 Turn the ends of the lace trim ¼" to the wrong side and stitch. Center the lace trim over the ribbon and stitch along both sides of trim. Tie the sash around the waist.

TIP

The lace with all white daisies trims the waist of the Spring Party Dress. The centers of the daisies in the skirt print are a dark jade green. I wanted to make the centers of the daisies on the lace match, so I colored the centers with a jade green fabric marker. If you will not be washing the garment, you can customize any daisy lace trim.

First Communion Dress and Veil

Supplies:
- ½ yd. white satin fabric
- ⅔ yd. lace fabric with a scalloped edge on both selvedges
- 1 yd. white satin ribbon (⅞" wide)
- 14" lace edging (⅝" wide)
- 3" Velcro strip
- ½ yard tulle
- 2¾" French clip barrette
- 1½ yd. white wired ribbon (1½" wide)
- Hot glue gun
- 10" or 11" dinner plate
- Rotary cutter

Ultimate Girls Club doll

Dress

1 Cut one 9" x 45" piece of satin fabric for the skirt. Cut one 9" x 22½" piece and two 9" x 11¼" pieces of lace fabric along each selvedge for the overskirt.

2 Cut one 4" x 20" piece of satin and lace fabric and one 3" x 20" piece of satin fabric. Place the wrong side of the lace over the right side of the wider satin and baste the long edges together. With right sides together, stitch both of the strips together along one long edge. Press the seam allowances open.

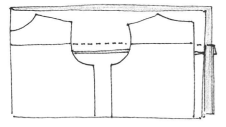

3 Place the back bodice pattern piece over the pieced fabric so that the fabric seam is under the line drawn on the pattern piece. Cut another back bodice piece

using the same method, but be sure to flip the pattern piece over. Fold the remaining fabric in half widthwise and cut the front bodice the same way. Cut one front lining, two back linings, and two sleeves from the satin fabric.

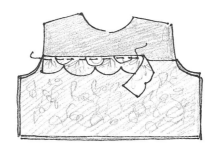

4 Place the lace edging over the yoke front seam on the right side of the front and stitch along the straight edge. Do the same with the lace over the yoke back seam on each back.

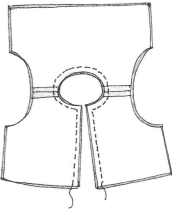

5 With right sides together, sew the shoulder seams of the dress front and backs. Press the seam allowances open. Repeat with the lining. Place the lining over the dress with right sides together. Stitch around the neckline and down each center back. Clip the curves, turn to the right side, and press. Baste around the armholes.

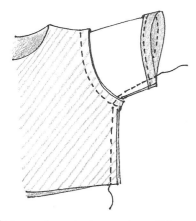

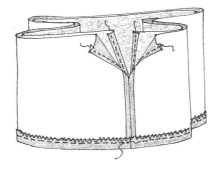

6 Narrow hem the lower edges of the sleeves. With right sides together, sew the sleeve caps to the armholes, easing as necessary. Stitch the underarm seams from the sleeve edges to the bottom of the bodice.

7 Serge or zigzag stitch one long edge of the satin skirt. Press this edge ½" to the wrong side and stitch. With right sides together, sew the short ends together to within 3" from the top. Press the seam allowances open, including the unstitched part, and top stitch around the opening.

8 With right sides together, sew the 11¼" lace skirt pieces to each side of the 22½" piece. Sew the 11¼" pieces from the scalloped edges to within 3" from the straight edge. Press the seam allowances open, including the unstitched part, and topstitch around the opening. Place the wrong side of the lace skirt to the right side of the satin skirt, lining up the top edges and the center back seam. From now on, the skirts will be treated as one.

9 Gather the top of the skirt to fit the bodice. With right sides together, stitch the skirt to the lower edge of the bodice.

10 Sew the Velcro to the back opening, lapping right over left.

11 Tie the ribbon around the waist.

Veil

1 Cut along the fold of the tulle along the 18" edge. Using the dinner plate and a rotary cutter, round all four edges of the tulle.

2 To give the veil a two-tiered appearance, fold the tulle edge so that there is 6" on top of 12". With a needle and thread run a gathering stitch along this folded edge. Gather the tulle to fit the 2¾" French clip barrette. Do not cut off gathering thread.

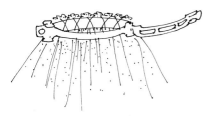

3 Remove the inside portion of the barrette for the following steps. Hot glue the tulle to the barrette. To insure that the tulle will not come off, use the gathering thread and bind the tulle to the barrette with six or seven stitches. Make sure that the end of gathering thread extends to the backside of the barrette. Do not cut off thread yet.

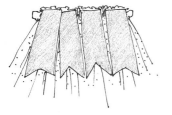

4 Cut four pieces of the wired ribbon to 6" long. Cut a notch at one end of each piece. Hot glue the four pieces, starting from the outside edge of the gathered tulle working toward the center.

Ultimate Girls Club doll

With the remaining ribbon, make a set of loops. The center loop should be about 1" with each succeeding loop being ½" larger. Hot glue each loop together until the entire unit is 3½" long. Hot glue the unit directly on top of the 6" pieces of ribbon and centered on the barrette.

5 With the gathering thread, bring the needle to the front of the veil and down inside the center loop, bringing the needle to the back of the veil at least three times. This gathers the ribbon at

the center and also secures the bow to the barrette. Knot the thread and clip close. Replace the inside piece of the barrette.

6 To make the veil fuller, carefully separate each piece of tulle working from the cut hem toward the barrette, pulling gently.

About the Author

This is Joan's eleventh book of patterns for 18-inch dolls! These books include a variety of costumes that range from playwear to ball gowns. In 1989, she and a former partner formed *Fancywork and Fashion*, a company that markets doll costuming, sewing books, sewing notions, and accessories. A quarterly newsletter is also published that features patterns and technique tips for the popular vinyl 18-inch doll.

Creating costumes and accessories for dolls is the perfect expression for Joan's love of sewing and design. All aspects of pattern drafting, fashion and interior design, embellishment, and fantasy are incorporated in projects that need only small amounts of fabric and trim. This book, *Sew Today's Fashions for 18-inch Dolls,* is the latest entry in her series of doll pattern books that feature current fashion and accessory trends for girls and their dolls.

Joan, a Minnesota native, travels the country to share her knowledge with sewing guilds, trade shows, and shops. Her work has been shown in *Designs in Machine Embroidery, Sew Beautiful, Doll Crafter,* and *Creative Needle* magazines. She has made an appearance on the PBS series, *America Sews with Sue Hausmann.*

Resources

Many of the craft items, fabrics, and accessories can be found at larger craft and sewing stores such as Michael's®, Hancock®, and Jo-Ann® stores. Dolls and accessories can be purchased from toy stores, mail-order companies, and some large retail outlets. The shoes shown in the photos can be obtained through many Web sites and mail-order companies.

Fancywork and Fashion
Joan Hinds
P.O. Box 3554
Duluth, MN 55803
(800) 365-5257
www.fancyworkandfashion.com
Sewing pattern books, accessories, doll sewing supplies including zippers, Dritz for Dolls® notions, and a quarterly newsletter with patterns for 18-inch dolls.

Krause Publications
700 E. State St.
Iola, WI 54990-0001
(800) 258-0929
www.krause.com

Dolls

American Girl® by Pleasant Company
8400 Fairway Place
P.O. Box 620190
Middleton, WI 53562-0190
(800) 845-0005
www.americangirl.com
Dolls, shoes, and accessories available by mail order only.

Götz® Dolls
This doll manufacturer has recently gone out of business, but dolls are still available in various toy stores around the country.

Our Generation® Dolls
Dolls and accessories are sold in Target® stores.

Ultimate Girls Club® Dolls
Dolls and accessories are sold in Shopko® stores.

Laura Ashley® Dolls
Dolls and accessories are sold in Toys "R" Us® stores.

Tolly Girl® Dolls by Tollytots, Inc.
Dolls and accessories are sold in Wal-Mart® stores.

Creative Doll®
Clotilde LLC
P.O. Box 7500
Big Sandy, TX 75755-7500
(800) 772-2891
www.clotilde.com
Dolls, shoes, sewing books, and notions.

Springfield Collection® Dolls by Fibre-Craft Materials Corp.
Dolls and accessories sold in Michael's® stores.

Shoes and Accessories

Doll manufacturers such as Pleasant Company®, Ultimate Girls Club®, Our Generation®, Laura Ashley®, Tolly Girl®, and the Springfield Collection® also sell accessories specifically designed for 18-inch dolls.

Abbey Creations
N5422 Abbey Rd.
Onalaska, WI 54650-9204
(608) 783-2398
www.abbeycreations.com

All About Dolls
72 Lakeside Blvd.
Hopatcong, NJ 07843
(800) 645-3655
www.allaboutdolls.com

All My Own, Inc.
9695 63rd Ave. North
Maple Grove, MN 55369
(888) 533-6557
www.allmyown.com

CR's Crafts
P.O. Box 8
Leland, IA 50453
(641) 567-3652
www.crscraft.com

Tallina's
15791 SE Hwy. 224
Clackamas, OR 97015
(503) 658-6148
www.dollsupply.com

TLC Doll
2479 Sheridan Blvd.
Edgewater, CO 80214
(888) 661-3655
www.tlcdoll.com

Sewing Notions
Prym-Dritz Corporation
www.dritz.com
(800) 255-7796 (customer service)
Products include eyelets, Easy-Bleach®, and Dritz for Dolls® notions including miniature fasteners, buckles, and ironing boards.

Machine Embroidery Designs
Cactus Punch, Inc.
4955 N. Shamrock Place
Tucson, AZ 85705
(800) 933-8081
www.cactuspunch.com
Designs used were from Sig88 Doll Clothing Designs by Joan Hinds.

Patterns

There are more patterns located on the pattern sheets inserted in the back of the book.

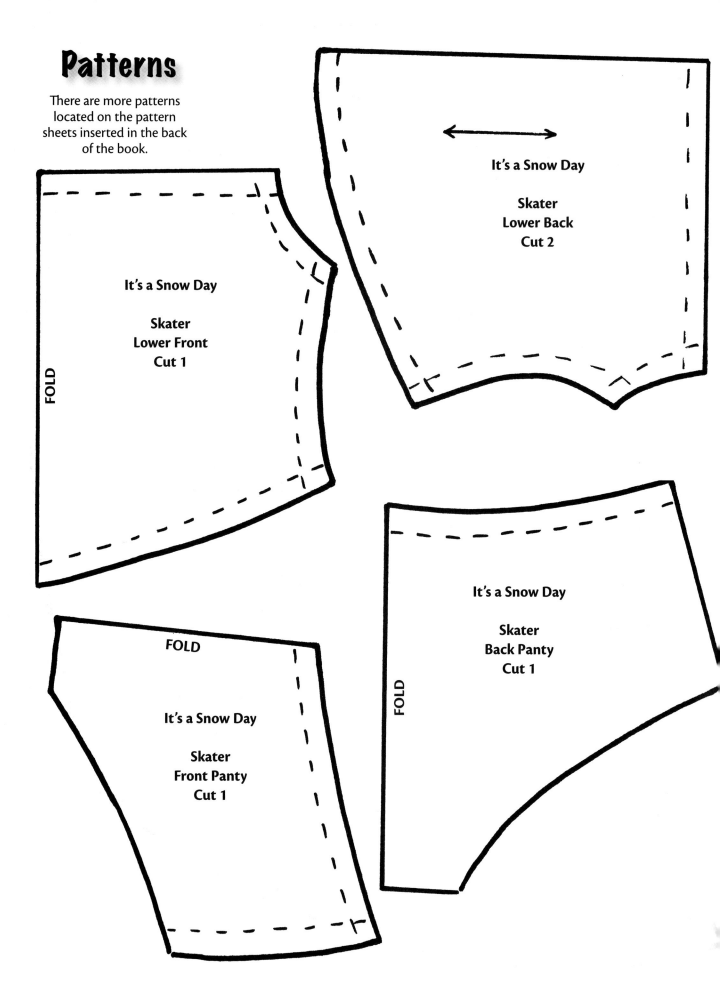

It's a Snow Day

Skater
Lower Front
Cut 1

FOLD

It's a Snow Day

Skater
Lower Back
Cut 2

FOLD

It's a Snow Day

Skater
Front Panty
Cut 1

It's a Snow Day

Skater
Back Panty
Cut 1

FOLD

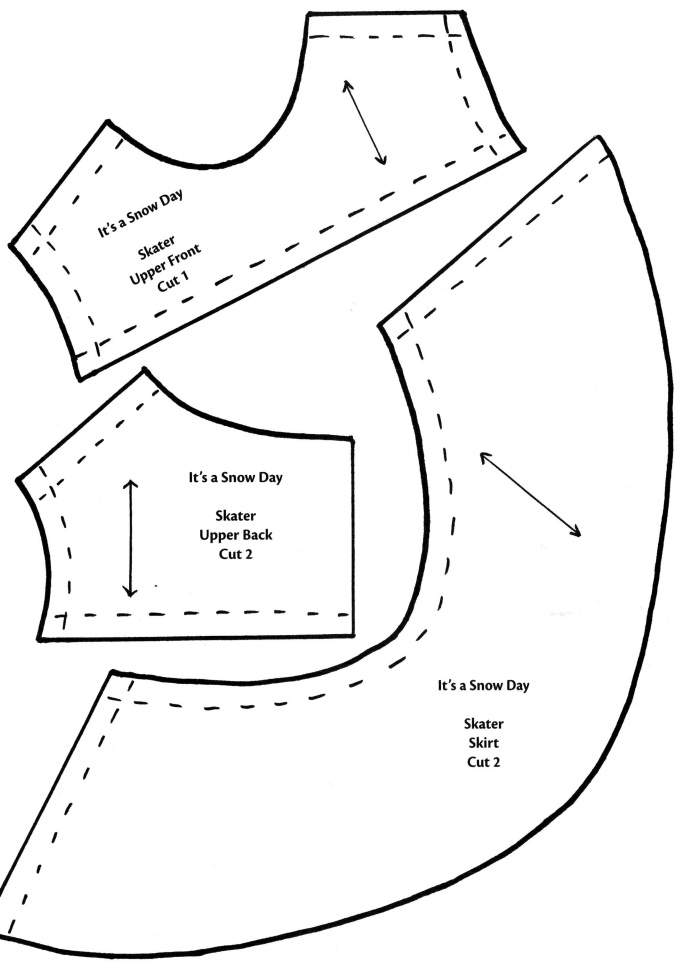

It's a Snow Day

Skater
Upper Front
Cut 1

It's a Snow Day

Skater
Upper Back
Cut 2

It's a Snow Day

Skater
Skirt
Cut 2

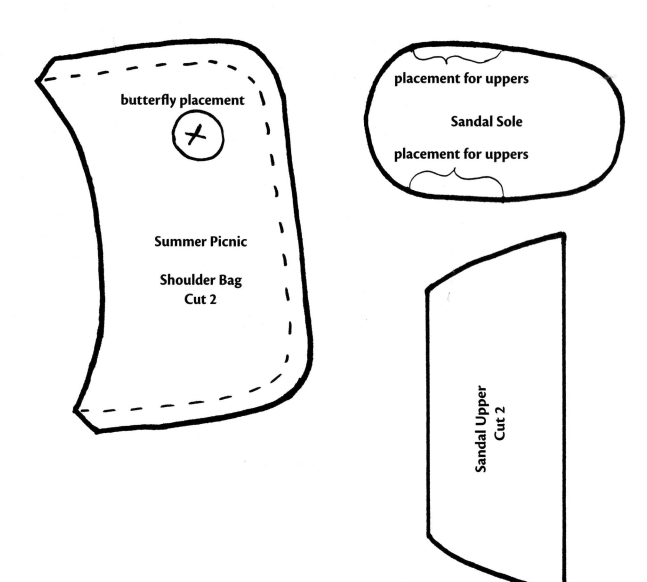

butterfly placement

Summer Picnic

Shoulder Bag
Cut 2

placement for uppers

Sandal Sole

placement for uppers

Sandal Upper
Cut 2